LEARNING AND TEACHING IN THE PRIMARY CLASSROOM

LEARNING AND TEACHING IN THE PRIMARY CLASSROOM

Maurice Galton

SAGE Publications

Los Angeles • London • New Delhi • Singapore

SAGE Publications Ltd
1 Oliver's Yard
55 City Road
London EC1Y 1SP

SAGE Publications Inc
2455 Teller Road
Thousand Oaks
California 91320

SAGE Publications India Pvt Ltd
B 1/I 1 Mohan Cooperative Industrial Area
Mathura Road
New Delhi 110 044

SAGE Publications Asia-Pacific Pte Ltd
33 Pekin Street #02-01
Far East Square
Singapore 048763

Library of Congress Control Number: 2006938166

A catalogue record for this book is available from the British Library

ISBN-978-1-4129-1834-3
ISBN-978-1-4129-1835-0 (pbk)

Typeset by Pantek Arts Ltd, Maidstone, Kent
Printed in Great Britain by TJ International, Padstow, Cornwall
Printed on paper from sustainable resources

Contents

List of Figures and Tables   vi

Introduction   xi

1 Primary teaching in contemporary settings   1

2 New Labour: New beginning?   13

3 Learning for teaching   30

4 Teaching for transmission and understanding   49

5 Making pupils metacognitively wise   71

6 Group work in the primary classroom   94

7 The social and emotional aspects of teaching and other matters   111

References   129

Index   145

List of Figures and Tables

Figures

2.1 KS2 national curriculum results (English) 1995–2005   16

2.2 KS2 national curriculum results (Mathematics) 1995–2005   17

2.3 Year 6 pupils' enjoyment of primary school   21

2.4 Open v. closed questions   26

3.1 A typology of knowledge acquisition   33

3.2 How pupils think and learn: working models   44

3.3 A classification of thinking skills   46

4.1 The concept of flow   51

4.2 Key steps in direct instruction   58

5.1 Knowledge, learning and pedagogy   75

5.2 Academic tasks   80

5.3 Knowledge, pedagogy and feedback   87

5.4 A possible cross-curriculum project plan   90

6.1 Example worksheet for dealing with behaviour problems   103

7.1 Example of a semi-rural primary school's discipline policy 115

Tables

Table 2.1 Year 6 pupils' attitudes to core subjects (2001–2005)   21

Table 2.2 The pattern of teachers' statements   26

Table 4.1 Instructional process for facilitating student learning   54

Table 4.2 Ten key features in teaching for understanding   67

Table 5.1 Effect sizes associated with various types of feedback   88

Table 6.1 Key phases of group work training   98

Acknowledgements

I would like to acknowledge the following sources for allowing me to use these extracts:

Dr. Adrienne Alton-Lee, Chief Educational Adviser of the New Zealand Ministry of Education, and the late Professor Graham Nuthall for permission to use part of a lesson transcript on cold fronts that is reproduced on pages 55–57.

Leicestershire County Council for permission to reproduce Figure 6.1 taken from their publication, *Out from Behind the Desk: A practical guide to groupwork skills and, processes*.

David Moseley, Director of the Learning and Skills Development Agency Project, *An Evaluation of Thinking Skill Taxonomies for post-16 Learners*, and colleagues at the University of Newcastle Upon Tyne, for permission to include Figure 3.3 which is based on their version in a paper given at an ESRC seminar and subsequently reproduced in a modified form in an article in the June 2005 edition of the British Educational Research Journal.

Dr K.K. Chan, Principal Assistant Secretary (Curriculum Development) Hong Kong Education and Manpower Board, for permission to incorporate part of Figure 5.4, which was taken from a draft of the Hong Kong *Senior Secondary Curriculum and Assessment Study Guide on Teaching and Learning*.

McGraw Hill for permission to use part of a transcript on page 61 illustrating wait time, which was taken from Chapter 8 of Mary Budd Rowe's book, *Teaching Science as Continuous Inquiry*.

To Matthew,
who had great primary teachers,
not-so-good secondary ones,
but came good in the end.

Introduction

This book is a sequel to one that I wrote some years ago on teaching in the primary class-room. In that book I tried to respond to the charges regarding poor teaching and the insistence by politicians that they had rescued schools from the ravages of the 1960s' progressive trends. At the same time I noted the increased pressure on primary teachers that had resulted from the introduction of the National Curriculum and the increased emphasis on testing. A sequel, *Crisis in the Primary Classroom* (1995), attempted to spell out the consequences of these policy initiatives on classroom pedagogy. Little did I think at the time that New Labour, despite increased funding, would make matters worse in many respects. The increased emphasis on a *performance* rather than a *learning* culture in our schools (one recent education minister told me that performance was the only acceptable measure of learning) has led to a drastic dip in pupil attitudes, a lowering of morale among teachers, an impoverished curriculum and a restricted pedagogy. Even the limited gains in so-called 'basics' (contested by other independent research studies) seem to have peaked in recent years. When excellent, dedicated teachers are leaving the profession because:

> 'After all my years in teaching I feel that my methods and opinions are worthless. With every new initiative we have to throw away other tried and tested methods that worked for us,'

and,

> 'I'm not looking for a career with more money; I'm looking for a career with more levels of satisfaction. I want to be challenged by things I want to be challenged by. At the moment I just feel challenged by everything and I want to be challenged by things which I feel have real value,'

while those who stay say:

> 'I wouldn't enter the profession now for £1,000 per week. It's stressful and socially destroying. I just love the children: that's why I continue,'[1]

then there is a serious problem of teacher professionalism which needs to be addressed urgently without recourse to the meaningless jargon and catch-all phrases to be found in much of the advice that emerges from the Department for Education and Skills Standards Unit and those responsible for coordinating the National Primary Strategy. Above all, teachers wish to regain control of pedagogy; the right to teach in ways which best promote the learning of the children in their charge, rather than adopting the rigid frameworks of the Literacy and Numeracy hours. There are signs that this battle is now being waged successfully, by some schools openly and by others stealthily. One difficulty is that for teachers under the age of 30, the National Curriculum and the associated targeting and testing regimes constituted their whole experience of schooling and teaching. There are, therefore, a decreasing number of practitioners who can remember what it was like before the reforms. Hence the purpose of this book: to set out some of the pedagogic principles that promote 'deep' rather than 'surface' learning and that encourage pupils to think for themselves.

For most of my career in education, spanning over 30 years, I have sat in the back of classrooms observing teachers teach and pupils learn. Beginning with the study of science teaching, then a series of studies over two decades following the ORACLE (Observational and Classroom Learning Evaluation) Project, the research has concerned such aspects as grouping and group work, curriculum provision in small schools, transfer to secondary school and, more recently, the way that artists, writers, dancers and actors motivate children who appear to lack the confidence to learn under normal classroom conditions. At times the research has involved working alongside teachers in order to gain better insights into what they did in the classroom and why they did it. I am grateful to the hundreds of teachers who allowed me the privilege of watching them teach and who were kind enough to spend precious time helping me better understand the complexities of daily classroom life. To my colleagues, in both Leicester and Cambridge, I also owe a debt of gratitude, but particularly to my collaborators in much of this research; Linda Hargreaves and Tony Pell, who have always been on hand to restrain me from more fanciful interpretations of the evidence. The views expressed here have been heavily influenced by their critical observations although I am, of course, responsible for what is set out on the following pages.

Additionally, at the end of each chapter I have given a list of key references for readers who want to follow up specific issues. These are also included in the References section at the end of the book.

Last, like many other authors, I have had trouble with current conventions. I have tried to avoid always referring to teachers in the singular as 'she' or 'her' unless it concerns a particular person, but confess defeat over the choice of student, child or pupil and have used each of these descriptors on various occasions.

Maurice Galton

---

[1]Quotations from *A Life in Teaching? The Impact of Change on Primary Teachers' Working Lives* by Maurice Galton and John MacBeath for the National Union of Teachers, June 2002.

Chapter 1

Primary Teaching in Contemporary Settings

Let us begin with brief descriptions of two recent visits to primary school classrooms that took place in the second half of the spring term. In the first school the Year 6 children have just been informed about the allocation of places in the local secondary schools to which they will transfer next autumn. Some of the class are clearly upset because they have not been given their first choice school and will therefore be separated from close friends at the start of the autumn term.

In this school it is readily apparent that there is an extremely strong emphasis on attainment in literacy and numeracy. On one of the Year 6 classroom walls a large triangle with several horizontal lines inserted is mounted. Above the diagram the title reads 'How many of these can you use correctly?'. On the smallest line, near the apex of the triangle, is written 'a comma = Level 1'. The next line states that 'comma + full stop = Level 2'. The third line has 'comma + full stop + speech marks = Level 3'. The class is divided into three groups. On the first table, which is set aside for those who already have reached Level 4, a former member of staff, recently retired, has been brought in for the second half of the year, and is working quietly with children on the use of speech marks. On the second table, children who are at present rated at Level 3 but thought to be able to reach a good Level 4 by May, are having work handed back to them by Mrs Clarke, the class teacher. She explains to one boy that linking several adjectives in his description would move his piece of writing into a Level 4 category and, as an example, suggests that he changes the sentence 'He walked along a narrow path' to 'He walked along a narrow, tree-lined, grassy path', remembering at the same time to add the commas. To a girl on the same table, she suggests that it would be a good thing to include some reported speech in the opening paragraph of her story so that she can demonstrate her knowledge about when to use speech marks. Under her guidance the girl adds an opening sentence:

'I think it's going to be a fine day,' said Tania's mother, looking up from her newspaper.

The third group, whom Mrs Clarke later describes in conversation as 'the no-hopers', is being looked after by a classroom assistant. These are children who will not reach Level 4 by May and are engaged in learning a list of spellings and the meaning of the words. Mrs Clarke says this is 'pretty much her standard lesson.' At the end of the visit the headteacher speaks admiringly of the improvement in the Year 6 national test scores since Mrs Clarke came to the school three years ago.

In another Year 6 classroom, not five miles away, Mr Vincent, the class teacher, has arranged the desks in two U-shapes. Children sit in friendship groups unless Mr Vincent decides that the chosen membership does not facilitate good working habits, in which case children are moved to another group. Because my visit is part of research into transfer from primary to secondary school, Mr Vincent decides to use the idea of transitions as a stimulus for the lesson. He tells the class that they are going to think about the future. Pupils are to construct a timeline of how they hope to develop as people over the next 20 years.

Before the class begin their task, Mr Vincent illustrates what he wants each pupil to do by telling them about his own youthful wishes and future hopes. He tells them that at their age he had three big ambitions: to go to college and be a teacher; to play football in a professional team and to go to Australia. Sadly, he has only managed to fulfil two of these three goals so far. He asks the children to guess which of his ambitions he has yet to achieve. One boy calls out to the accompaniment of general laughter:

'Professional football player. You were useless trying to save our penalties last week.'

The children then spend time in the groups discussing various ideas before they are instructed to draw their own timelines and to write their accounts with reasons for their choices. There then ensues a lively class discussion where each pupil is asked to share their ideas with the rest of the class. Mr Vincent makes great efforts to open up the discussion by not always responding immediately whenever a pupil finishes speaking. Sometimes, however, he is drawn into making a response by the surprising nature of the answers. For example, Donna tells the class that her three ambitions placed on her timeline are, first, to go to college, second, have two children and third, to get married.

Mr Vincent: 'Don't you mean getting married and then having two children?'
Donna (with great firmness) 'No. I don't.'

Afterwards Mr Vincent explains to me that although he was influenced in his choice of topic by the research theme, he often chooses to do things 'out of the blue' and not to follow the normal literacy hour lesson. In the course of this conversation he expresses the view that:

'I don't think it is helpful for children of this age to have their creativity and imagination stifled by having to follow set prescriptions. Learning is best done by doing. And I don't think that banging on about full stops and commas and different kinds of writing genres helps children to develop their minds.'

This opinion is in sharp contrast to Mrs Clarke's view. She likes the literacy hour because it gives a firm structure to her teaching and the pupils know what they have to do to succeed. Furthermore, some of the materials produced by the Qualifications and Curriculum Authority (QCA) are very useful because they:

'Save you the trouble of having to plan lessons. It cuts out the need to think and allows more time for marking.'

Teaching dichotomies

The point in starting with these two brief vignettes is to highlight a fundamental weakness in the current debates on pedagogy. For as long as the subject of teaching methods has been discussed, and you could read a text on educational psychology in the 1960s and not find the word 'teaching' mentioned in the entire index, the tendency has been to polarise issues in terms of two extreme positions. Initially, teachers were said to adopt traditional practices, which it was claimed were based on the behavioural theories of Skinner, or they espoused a 'child-centred', 'progressive' approach which took its inspiration from the earlier ideas of Rousseau and Pestalozzi that were later grounded in the developmental psychology of Jean Piaget by the likes of Susan and Nathan Issacs. At various times this debate about the effectiveness of these teaching methods might have been conducted using alternative terminologies such as 'transmission v. discovery' approaches or, more recently, 'active v. passive' learning. But the underlying assumption with all these dichotomies appeared to be that there was a clear choice to be made and that a teacher must belong to one camp or the other. When most teachers responded by claiming that they used a mix of the two approaches, it was rare to find among practitioners anyone able to explain the rationale for choosing one approach rather than the other on a particular occasion. Furthermore, for many experienced primary teachers and a good number of those responsible for their initial training, such questions about a theoretical basis for the choice of teaching method was a non-issue, since the second 'law of pedagogy' was often expressed by the view that:

'There is no one best way to teach so that teachers choose approaches that they feel comfortable with and which work.'

A scientific approach to teaching?

The above justifications for everyday practice, however, do not operate in other disciplines, particularly in the physical sciences. It is true that in science there are heated debates over the rightness or wrongness of theories, as for example about the origins of the universe, and in much the same way educational psychologists will dispute theories of learning. Part of the outcome of such debates in science, and indeed all disciplines, is to develop new paradigms which will subsume different theories of an earlier generation. But this approach to theorising applies to what one might term 'big science', and involves the most creative thinkers who are working at the frontiers of their specialism. The world of science (and psychology), however, is made up of many other practitioners who are not such expert thinkers and innovators. These people are content to fill in the contours in the hinterland rather than working at the frontiers of knowledge in their specialism. In doing so they make use of any appropriate existing theory or model which solves the problems they have to deal with.

Such scientists are likely, for example, to use a wave theory when dealing with problems concerning the transmission of sound in the atmosphere but a particle approach when the problem involves the transmission of heat by conduction. They leave it to the more advanced thinkers to use increasingly sophisticated models in order to produce more rounded 'intellectually satisfying' solutions. Thus there is a clear distinction between the use of what may be termed 'working theories' which can be used to solve a myriad of problems that explain everyday phenomena operating at a macro level and the search for 'unifying theories' that are required to make sense of our universe at a sub-atomic, micro level.

The tendency to use a 'working theory' approach most often occurs in the case of practical applications. In the same way this book will propose that pedagogy can also have a 'scientific basis' but that teachers need only to adopt a 'working theory' approach when seeking to use ideas about learning as a rationale for choosing one teaching method rather than another. A dilemma such as whether to favour a 'traditional' or 'progressive' stance is therefore to be regarded as a non-question (even if it were possible to define such broad all-embracing constructs in precise operational terms). Neither is it useful to attempt, as has New Labour with their literacy and numeracy strategies, to create an all-purpose, all-embracing unified approach that combines the presumed strengths of different methods in the way that *whole class interactive teaching* attempts to do. The perspective that will be adopted here is that the most appropriate strategy is to take a 'horses for courses' approach in matters of pedagogy. In choosing a particular teaching method we should do so because it works in relation to the tasks which we wish children to perform. Teaching a class the basis of English grammar requires a different teaching strategy to that used in helping pupils to become creative writers. In each case we need to draw on different theories (or models) of learning in our search for the most appropriate teaching approach.

In constructing a scientific basis for teaching, we can obviously make use of theories of learning derived from psychology in the main, but we need also to couple this knowledge with empirical data mainly derived from classroom observation studies. Interestingly, just as there has been a tendency to polarise the debate about effectiveness of different teaching approaches, so too there has been a similar heated debate about whether teaching is, uniquely, an art or a science and, if the latter, open therefore to systematic enquiry. For Woods (1996) it is indisputably an art. Those who take this position adhere to the view that teachers develop their practice mainly through a process of intuition (Claxton 2000) coupled with regular periods of self-reflection, rather than by making use of theoretically-based knowledge, or what Schon terms *technical rationality*. According to Schon, 'problems of real world practice do not present themselves to practitioners as well formed structures' (1987: 3–4). In recent years, therefore, the notion that there is an objective body of knowledge about teaching that can determine effective practice has come under increasing criticism from a variety of perspectives, although as Furlong (2000) argues, the lack of any consensus regarding an alternative approach has helped to create a crisis in teacher professionalism.

New Labour, new pedagogy?

New Labour has sought to deal with this crisis by promoting what has come to be generally known as 'evidence-based practice'. One ex-government spokesman, Michael Barber (2002), the former head of the Standards Agency, argues that teaching moved through four main cycles during the second half of the 20th century. The first of these cycles, covering the period up to Mrs Thatcher's election as Prime Minister in 1979, was largely based on teachers' personal intuitions (or as some have claimed, personal prejudices) and was one of *uninformed professionalism*. This was replaced during the 18 years of Conservative rule by *uninformed prescription*, where, for example, the so-called integrated day was always bad and organising teaching by subjects automatically good. When New Labour came to power in 1997 it was therefore necessary, according to Barber, to correct the errors of the previous government so that a period of *informed prescription* was necessary. In the main this involved a somewhat rigid imposition of the literacy and numeracy strategies in primary schools. Now, however, with the decline in standards halted, it has been possible at the start of the new millennium to enter a period of *informed professionalism* where teachers can access, through the Internet, relevant Ofsted reviews and the latest EPPI (Evidence for Policy and Practice Information) surveys in order to inform their classroom decision making.

It is a reassuring view of the present situation but, unfortunately, one without much foundation. As Everton *et al*. (2002) demonstrated, there tends to be a gap of nearly 10 years between teachers' awareness of research and its publication. Furthermore, it is not clear why research which is methodologically strong and which is consistent in its results, the kind which is rated highly in EPPI reviews, appears to hold less attraction for teachers than other offerings such as *learning styles*, or *left brain–right brain training* procedures such as 'Brain Gym' for which the research evidence is far less strong or negligible. In any case, the debate between those who view teaching as mainly an art based on intuition and reflection, and those calling for a scientific approach to be determined from evidence-based practice, often fail to recognise that they are referring to different levels of decision making when teaching a given topic to a particular class.

Any theory must have general applications: if it were too specific it would be of little use. In teaching, as in many other practical applications where one is not in total control of the situation, the application of any set of principles (the theory) therefore must be varied to suit the particular set of circumstances defining the given context. For example, there is a body of research strongly supporting the principle that pupils need thinking time when faced with challenging questions. Consider a novice teacher who attempts to put this principle into practice by pausing for at least three seconds after formulating the question and is faced by a barrage of children with their hands up shouting out 'Ask me, sir! Ask me!' Quickly losing control, he is told by his teacher mentor that it is essential not to let the pace of the lesson drop off and that questioning should therefore always involve rapid exchanges between teachers and pupils. Elsewhere, in another classroom, a more experienced, reflective practitioner has enacted the same principle by telling her pupils that there are lots of answers to the question she has posed and that she wants them to talk for a few minutes among themselves before she will listen to their responses. The resulting discussion is lively and pupils show evidence of higher order thinking. The difference in approach was not only determined by the depth of the second teacher's knowledge (either from intuition or from previous experience) that longer pauses would result in disruption, it was also conditioned by the nature of this teacher's relationship with her pupils (developed over time) in that she was reasonably sure the class would concentrate on the task when they were told to talk among themselves. The novice teacher would have been unlikely to have been able to guarantee such certainty and would therefore have been reluctant to relinquish control of the situation. As argued by Anderson and Burns (1989) in their Preface:

> Contrary to some people's opinions, evidence does not speak for itself. The translation of evidence into thought and action requires people who understand both the research and the classroom.

This viewpoint reflects the distinction formulated by the psychologist, Nate Gage, over 30 years ago when he argued that pedagogy was the science of the art of teaching (Gage 1978). In any discipline there must be principles based on theoretical perspectives and empirical evidence. But such principles need to be adjusted to meet the particular conditions in which teachers find themselves.

The science of the art of teaching

Robin Alexander (2000) introduces a further caveat into this debate. He contests both the rather rigid notion of teaching as a science adopted by those such as David Reynolds and others in the school effectiveness movements (Reynolds 2000) who appear to believe that pedagogy can be reduced to a series of laws. However, Alexander also rejects the view of Woods (1996) in arguing that teaching should be regarded solely as an art. He prefers instead the ideas expressed by Gage, that there is a scientific component which consists of general principles that then have to be situated in the context of individual teachers' class-rooms. As such it must encompass the kind of knowing and understandings about matters such as the balance between group work and whole class teaching in the course of a lesson. Alexander, however, argues that these latter decisions are much more to do with the accumulated wisdom which teachers acquire as they gain experience that allows them to make judgements about the *fitness for purpose* of particular actions within a particular context. This kind of knowledge Alexander terms *craft knowledge*. Desforges offers a similar perspective but observes that since much of this professional knowledge is 'generated behind the closed doors of an individual teacher's classroom it is rarely written down and consequently it is difficult to articulate'. He contends that:

> Schools could be even more successful than they are now in promoting achievement if we could all learn to share and use the knowledge we have now about learning. I recognise that there is a vast body of knowledge about learning evident in the everyday practices of teachers. This knowledge is difficult to get at and so it is difficult to share. There is also a small but strong body of scientific knowledge about learning to be gleaned from research. This knowledge is easy to get at but difficult to apply. The trick we need to perform is to bring the practical knowledge and the theoretical knowledge together to promote advanced teaching practices. (2003: 15–16)

To conclude this discussion, therefore, there is a certain degree of truth about the statement that teachers know best how to teach, because over time teachers do build up a range of strategies they can draw upon. This situation comes about because these experienced practitioners have used this strategy successfully when faced with similar situations in the past. But teaching is also artistic, in the sense that it is creative, because it is rare that two classroom situations are exactly alike and some teachers are able, partly through intuition, to 'tweak' a particular teaching approach so that it works in a particular context. Some teachers are thus able to teach successfully mainly through a mixture of intuition and craft knowledge. Elsewhere, Galton (1995: 145) has described one such teacher whose practice exemplified theories of motivation of which she was totally unaware. But for others, who do not have such natural talent, teaching is likely to become stultified if too great a reliance is placed upon craft knowledge. This is because when facing new challenges such teachers will have little recourse but to cast their minds back through numerous past occasions in order to determine a maxim or rule which they feel meets the current situation. In such cases those of us who are merely competent and proficient rather than expert need to be able to draw on some principles of teaching. And it is in this sense that there needs to be a scientific basis to our pedagogy.

Our confidence in such principles grows, however, when a form of 'triangulation' is arrived at in which theoretical principles, the empirically observed practice and the teacher's craft knowledge, concur. It is the claim of those who engage in the study of classroom that over the last 50 years sufficient evidence has been accumulated mainly in the United States but also in the United Kingdom about which particular approaches are most suited for certain forms of learning. It is the aim of this book to elaborate on these principles.

At the same time it is important to recognise that compared to other disciplines the scientific study of teaching is in its infancy. Charles Desforges attempts to put the extent of our knowledge about teaching in context by stating that 'we know as much about learning as Sir Issac Newton knew about motion in the 17th century when he set out his celebrated laws' (2003:1). Even so, as Desforges goes on to point out, Newton's laws have proved their worth over time, as in the development of rockets for space exploration. Indeed, there are those who now claim that the ability to see inside the human brain, through the use of various scanning techniques, has brought the study of educational psychology to a point where it is on the verge of a similar scientific revolution to that which took place when Einstein began to replace Newtonian physics by the more comprehensive theory of relativity. Although, therefore, the study of teaching and learning is in an early stage of development, it nevertheless has established some important principles that can usefully ground present-day classroom practice.

What it is to teach

So far, however, we have tended to use terms like 'teaching', 'methods', 'approaches', 'pedagogy', as if they were all interchangeable. It is perhaps useful, at this point, to try to clarify such terms mainly by using the detailed analysis carried out by Robin Alexander (2000). As Anderson and Burns (1989: 4) note, teaching has usually been defined, historically, as the imparting of knowledge or skill. This definition, however, begs the question of effectiveness since it could be that the teacher attempts to impart knowledge but that the pupils do not absorb this information, or if they do, fail to retain it. In attempting to arrive at a more elaborate definition Good (1973), for example, argues that it is the intention of the teacher that matters, so that as long as pupils make an attempt to learn this is sufficient to indicate that teaching has occurred. Teaching is therefore not only a matter of providing instruction, but it also presumes intent on the part of the teacher that he or she is attempting to achieve some specific goal. For Good (1973), teaching is therefore an *intentional* as well as an *interpersonal* activity or process which leads Anderson and Burns to define teaching as 'an interpersonal, interactive activity typically involving verbal communication, which is undertaken for the purpose of helping one or more students learn or change the ways in which they can or will behave' (1989: 8).

For Alexander (2000: 323–4), a starting position is that teaching is an act of using Method X to enable pupils to learn Y. However, Alexander accepts that this definition subsumes a further set of questions to do with: (a) the nature of the learning task that the pupils are asked to undertake; (b) the activities that the teacher chooses in order to address these tasks; (c) the judgements that teachers have to make about the levels of such tasks which different pupils undertake; and (d) the kinds of outcomes on which the teacher will judge the success or failure of this activity. These judgements are sustained through a series of teacher–pupil interactions. When therefore these further questions are taken into consideration, then Alexander's definition is not so dissimilar from that proposed by Anderson and Burns.

The position taken throughout this book, however, seeks to extend the above framework in arguing that teaching is both an intentional and unintentional activity. This is because only part of teaching involves conscious decision making. This follows from a distinction made some years ago by the psychologist Gordon Allport (1966), who argued that a person's actions consist not only of a coping or rational responses to external events but also of an expressive response based on our emotions. Because teaching is also an emotional as well as an intentional activity (Hargreaves 2001), the approaches that we *intentionally* choose often become modified during lessons so that what teachers think they are doing often conflicts with the impressions of an impartial observer. Thus, as teachers, we may intentionally close down the range of questions we had intended to put to children because we wish to pursue a particular line of enquiry, although subsequently we may maintain, as for example in the Ford Teaching Project (Elliott 1976), that children were given the opportunity to consider a range of possible alternatives. Since all definitions of teaching accept that the interactions taking place between the pupils and the teacher in order to achieve desired learning outcomes is a key factor, then the possibility that these interactions are not always intentional must be considered. The situation is further complicated because once we accept that teaching is, in part, an emotional activity, then so is learning from the pupil's point of view; interactions between pupils and teachers are therefore continually operating at two levels. When we record these interactions (in whatever way) and then ask participants (teachers and pupils) for their explanations of these classroom events, we must be careful, as outsiders to the action, not to assume that these teacher and pupil accounts constitute the only explanation for the observed behaviours. One of the problems of 'top-down' curriculum development as practised by recent governments in the United Kingdom is that they rarely concern themselves with anything other than the rational, intentional view of teaching, and are thus often unable to comprehend why teachers fail to put into practice the curriculum as they, the developers, intended. Usually such failures are seen as the fault of recalcitrant teachers with the result, as in the case of New Labour, that more prescriptive forms of curriculum are devised.

Teaching and subject knowledge

It follows therefore that if teaching is primarily an interactive process, then pedagogy carries with it a wider connotation. Yet the definitions proposed by Watkins and Mortimore (1999) that pedagogy has its focus on both teaching and learning is little different from the more elaborate definitions of teaching employed by both Anderson and Burns (1989) and by Robin Alexander. Alexander (2000: 541–7) is again helpful here by suggesting that while most definitions of pedagogy encompass both the theory and practice of teaching, there are differences between our (mainly UK and USA) tradition and that of Central Europe. In Continental European countries 'pedagogy' is the more general term which encompasses both theoretical and practical aspects of teaching and learning, while the term 'didactics' is used to refer to that branch of pedagogy which deals specifically with what is to be taught and how. In particular, didactics tends to concentrate on different approaches across subjects rather than the general principles of teaching where the term 'pedagogy', is more often used. This has interesting connotations with the situation in England where, until recently, discussions about primary pedagogy (or teaching) generally assumed that the methods recommended were universally applicable no matter what was being taught. However, recently the introduction of the notion of 'subject content pedagogy' (Shulman 1987) has been predicated on the ideas developed by philosophers of education in the 1960s, who argued that the essential characteristics of any discipline were that it could establish a claim to invoke particular procedures in an attempt to establish or verify the truth of any given proposition (Hirst 1968). Thus for Shulman (1987) each subject has its own special compendium of useful analogies and its own methods of conducting enquiries. Expert teachers are those who developed superior subject knowledge of this kind.

It is important, however, to recognise that Shulman's emphasis on the importance of subject knowledge developed in reaction to the ideas of Harnischfeger and Wiley (1978), who argued that time on task was the main determinant of pupils' learning. Shulman was concerned to defend the traditional view of disciplined knowledge and argued that it was not so much the time that pupils spent on instruction but the quality of the instruction which was the determining factor. Part of the unease of many teachers in today's primary classrooms is that Shulman's view has led to an over-emphasis on subject knowledge in recent government initiatives (including the prescription of specific teaching approaches) to the detriment of more general ideas about learning, which are derived mainly from psychological theories. In this connection, Robin Alexander (2000) observes that Continental European countries such as Germany and Russia, although they make a distinction between what might be termed general didactics and specialist subject didactics, nevertheless endeavour to encompass the two in their analysis of teaching and pedagogy in an attempt to incorporate wider issues to do with child development, motivation, and other aspects of social learning.

The present status of pedagogy

In summary, therefore, in attempting to set the scene, it has been argued that teaching must encompass a set of general principles which might be equated to a 'science of teaching' but that these principles have to be adapted to suit different classroom contexts (the art of teaching). Furthermore, we have argued that teaching is not only an intentional activity but also an unintentional one because it works on both a cognitive and an emotional level and the latter aspect gives rise to actions which are often unrecognised by the practitioner. There is a further aspect of teaching which derives from experience of what works in practice, which we may term *craft knowledge*. In seeking to verify key aspects of pedagogy, that is integration of both theory and practice, we should strive to build up a consensus around theories derived from the educational disciplines (mainly psychology), empirical evidence, collected largely on the basis of classroom observation, and teachers' craft knowledge. Finally we need to be aware that while certain aspects of pedagogy may refer specifically to a subject or a discipline, there are nevertheless more general principles, which carry across different subjects and inform our ideas not only about learning but also about other factors which influence pupil behaviour, such as motivation and self-esteem. It is this latter aspect of pedagogy, concerning these more general principles of teaching, that is the main concern of this book.

In some areas considerable progress in establishing this consensus has already been made. Classroom research in the 1970s (Good and Grouws 1979 in mathematics and Anderson *et al.* 1979 in reading) established specific rules for effective teaching, which were generalised by Rosenshine (1979) for the Beginning Teacher Education Study (BTES) as 'direct instruction'. Furthermore, in contrast to popular myth that the 1960s had resulted in a revolution in teaching methods so that children 'were left to find out things for themselves', observation studies such as Galton *et al.* (1980) clearly demonstrated that for the most part when teaching mathematics or English, to what were then termed 'junior age pupils', teachers acted as instructors rather than as facilitators in most lessons. There appeared therefore to be general agreement between what theory suggested, classroom research had established, and what practitioners were observed to do in the matter of teaching the so-called basic skills of numeracy and literacy. The case for making this approach mandatory, as suggested by Reynolds (2000) particularly in respect of new entrants to the profession during their training, would seem to be a strong one.

Nevertheless, those who conceive of pedagogy as 'the science of the art of teaching' oppose such an approach mainly on the grounds that it is a *technical* rather than a *professional* solution to what over two decades ago Lortie (1975) identified as the 'conservative' nature of teaching. The term *conservatism* was chosen to describe a central feature of the culture of teaching in which practitioners tend to avoid engaging in discussions on matters of teaching and learning beyond a superficial level for fear it may raise fundamental questions about their existing practice. For this reason many teachers are often reluctant to engage in forms of collaboration with colleagues, such as team teaching, unless evidence exists that the colleagues' views on classroom practice are similar to their own. This is what Lortie characterised as a culture of *individualism* which in turn leads to *presentism*, the tendency of teachers to concentrate on short-term planning in their own classrooms where their efforts can be seen to have an immediate impact.

The resistance of this culture to change is further reinforced because the ideas, values and beliefs associated with particular practices become identified with the group rather than individuals. Terms such as 'good primary practice', for example, not only come 'to identify but to define, justify and control' membership of the primary teaching community (Alexander 1992: 169). In seeking reward for effective teaching, individuals must demonstrate 'cultural purity' by visibly acting out the ideas and values of the group with which they identify. Hargreaves makes a similar point when distinguishing between the *content* and the *form* of a culture: the former he defines as the system of shared beliefs in a community and the latter as 'the pattern of relationships and forms of association between members of that culture' (1992: 219). For Hargreaves, it is these cultural forms which are most resistant to change.

Those wishing to impose solutions either in matters of pedagogy or curriculum without taking into account the complex nature of the interplay between ideas and structure therefore run the risk that, in all probability, their suggested solutions will be applied uncritically and in ways which cause minimum disturbance to existing practice. Thus in the UK, consistent pressure has been exerted upon primary teachers in recent years to reduce the amount of individual attention given to pupils, and to engage in more whole-class 'interactive' teaching. The consequence of both *individualism* and *presentism* on this injunction can be demonstrated in the replication of the ORACLE carried out two decades later. In the late 1970s, 72 per cent of primary teachers' interactions were with individual pupils and only 19% were with the whole class (Galton *et al.* 1980). By 1996–97, when the replication study took place, the corresponding figures were 48.4 per cent and 35.2 per cent respectively (Galton *et al.* 1999). But when the nature of the teacher–pupil interaction was examined, it appeared that despite a major shift in organisational strategy little had changed. Whereas in 1976–77 teachers used 3.7 times as many statements as questions, by 1996–97 this ratio had only been marginally reduced to 3.6. Teachers therefore still mainly talked *at* rather than *with* their pupils and appeared to have taken a line of least resistance and merely 'bolted' existing practice onto the prescribed changes in classroom organisation. Furthermore, these imposed changes had a negative effect on the attitudes of teachers. For the most part, according to Woods *et al.* (1997) ten years of imposed reform in the UK has resulted in most teachers becoming 'less engaged' and 'committed'. Woods and his colleagues found that while few were actively hostile, other teachers said they conformed to survive and compensated by increasing their interests outside of teaching. Under New Labour these views have, if anything, intensified (Galton and MacBeath 2002). As one teacher interviewed by Woods *et al.* stated, 'There is no reason for me to be here now except to collect a pay cheque' (1997: 67). Such teachers increasingly see teaching as a *technical* activity, where the justification for doing *this* rather than *that* stems from the regulations rather than a pupil's needs. They therefore feel diminished both as individuals and as members of their professional group.

To bring about effective change in a way that enhances the teacher's sense of professionalism therefore requires both the *content* and *form* of the teaching culture to be modified. The starting point must be to switch attention away from the New Labour government's obsession with performance within national and international league tables and to concentrate, instead, on attempts to achieve a better understanding of how pupils learn and how this knowledge impacts on teaching. This book was conceived as a contribution to this attempt by some in education to shift the current debate away from its current emphasis on *performance* towards greater understanding of the way that pupils learn and the implications of this knowledge for teaching. However, before moving to a discussion of these issues the record of New Labour will be reviewed in order to substantiate the claim that a shift away from the current policies and practices that operate in today's primary schools is now an urgent necessity.

Key references

Alexander, R. (2000) *Culture and Pedagogy: International Comparisons of Primary Education*, Oxford: Blackwell. Part IV Classrooms, pp. 263–529.

Claxton, G. (2000) The anatomy of intuition, in Atkinson, T. and Claxton, G. (eds) *The Intuitive Practitioner: On the Value of not always Knowing what one is Doing*, Buckingham: Open University Press.

Desforges, C. (2003) On learning and teaching, in *Learning Texts*, a series of papers published by National College for School Leadership, www.ncsl.org.uk

Woods, P. (1996) *Researching the Art of Teaching*, Abingdon: Routledge.

Chapter 2

New Labour: New Beginning?

In a previous book written just before New Labour was about to take power the hope was expressed that these 'futon socialists' would undo some of the damage which had ensued during the last decade of Conservative rule (Galton 1995). However, the manifesto promise of education, education, education got off to an unpromising start when the new Secretary of State for Education began by naming and shaming 'the 18 worst schools in the country'. As reported by Liz Lightfoot, the then education correspondent of the *Daily Telegraph*.

> Special consultants with proven records of turning schools round are to be sent in. Their £400-a-day fees will be paid by the Government. David Blunkett, the Education Secretary, gave warning that those who failed to raise standards would be closed and re-opened under a new name and possibly a new headteacher and change of staff. (Lightfoot 1997)

At the time, supporters of the then recently elected government tended to attribute this initiative to the political climate which required New Labour to be seen to be as tough on standards as its predecessor. They argued that as the government gained in confidence it would begin to roll back some of the more regressive measures passed during Conservative rule which a recent survey indicated had so demoralised teachers (Galton and Fogelman 1998).

The purpose of this chapter is therefore to assess how far the aspirations of these supporters have been fulfilled as a starting point for a re-examination of current classroom practice. Are primary teachers happier and more satisfied with their job? Are pupils doing better and do they have greater aptitude towards learning? Have, as it is claimed, teaching methods improved? Has all the money which has gone into the system – and a lot of money *has* been injected into primary schools – produced the desired results?

Reforming the reform

Writing in the Introduction to a book setting out views of what it was hoped New Labour would do in the field of education, Sheila Dainton (1998), a senior official in the Association for Teachers and Lecturers (ATL), expressed the hope that the review of the National Curriculum promised by the Secretary of State for Education would be the last for a very long time. As set out in the opening paragraph to this chapter, Mr Blunkett's start was not auspicious. Although committed to a review of the National Curriculum (following the ending of the Dearing 5-year moratorium) and reminding primary teachers that they were required to develop a 'balanced and broadly based curriculum' and to promote the 'spiritual, moral, cultural, mental and physical development of pupils', he nevertheless announced a number of measures which it was claimed would ensure that primary teachers continued to focus on basics in order to meet the government's challenging literacy and numeracy targets. The retention of Chris Woodhead as Chief Inspector was also not calculated to reassure the profession. Despite numerous warnings that the previous decade had produced a profession suffering from 'reform fatigue' (Campbell 1998: 96), New Labour, in their first year of office, according to Tomlinson (2005) produced seven major bills and policy statements. As far as primary education was concerned, the most significant of these initiatives included the setting up of the Standard and Effectiveness Unit inside the DfEE, the launch of the 'New Deal' with the Summer Literacy Schools Initiative, the White Paper *Excellence in Schools* (DfEE 1997) in which the National Literacy Strategy was announced (including a decision to devote one hour a day to literacy in all primary schools) and the Schools Standards and Frameworks Bill. This was followed in the second year of office in 1998 by the setting up of Educational Action Zones, the National Grid for Learning, the setting up of the Numeracy Taskforce, the publication of homework guidelines, the launching of Surestart programmes for the 0 to 3-year-olds in areas of deprivation and the creation of Specialist and Beacon schools for inner cities. This raft of government initiatives, new Acts, new bodies (mostly consisting of nominated quangos or task forces), new green and white papers has continued apace throughout New Labour's rule. As far as primary schools were concerned, most commentators (Chitty 2004; Tomlinson 2005; Walford 2005) would agree that the important events concerned the introduction of the National Literacy and Numeracy Strategies, designed to ensure that all primary pupils met agreed targets, and the priority given to the disadvantaged through the Educational Action Zones which later were incorporated into the framework of *Excellence in Cities* (DfEE 1999).

Brehony (2005) has attempted to evaluate the impact of these policies, in their broadest sense, on primary schools. He notes that the thinking behind the Literacy and Numeracy Strategies appears to have had its origin in the 'third way' developed by President Clinton and the Democratic Party in the United States. While under previous Conservative rule, central government had attempted to mandate teachers to adopt certain teaching methods; in promoting these new strategies (particularly the literacy one) New Labour took matters considerably further.

One of the final acts of the Conservative government was to set up the National Literacy Project in 1996. The Framework for Teaching endorsed by the project incorporated a dedicated literacy teaching time of one hour per day and a structure of class management which shunned individualised approaches in favour of whole-class teaching. The emphasis on the 'back to basics' policy advocated by the then Chief Inspector, Chris Woodhead, meant that there was an increase in the mechanics of reading and writing with greater emphasis on both phonics and grammar.

Both Professor Michael Barber, with responsibility for literacy, and Professor David Reynolds, who headed the National Numeracy Taskforce, were products of the school improvement movement. In the same way that the Literacy Taskforce emphasised grammar and the mechanics of writing, so the numeracy group gave a similar priority to calculation skills. In both cases the focus was on whole-class teaching largely based on the various reviews by Ofsted, including one by Reynolds himself (Reynolds and Farrell 1996). Others, however, have challenged the claim that both the literacy and numeracy strategies represented the best 'evidence-based practice' (Brown *et al.* 1998), while Alexander (2004: 22) points out that the review of evidence on literacy, for example, was only compiled after the literacy hour was made a statutory requirement when Beard (1998) finally produced his review.

Subsequently, national targets were set such that by the year 2002, 80 per cent of 11-year-olds would reach the expected standard for their age in English and 75 per cent would reach this level in mathematics. In successive years, however, considerable concern has been expressed about the rigidity of the strategies. Schools struggled to come to terms with the question of how to fit the rest of the curriculum into the timetable, given that 10 hours of the 25 hours of primary schooling per week were now taken up by mathematics and English. According to Brehony anxieties were expressed elsewhere in government 'that an overly dirigiste approach to the management of teachers and an overly explicit classroom pedagogy would do little to release the creativity and innovation which the knowledge-based economy would require' (2005: 39). Others such as Bentley (1998), then a director of the think-tank DEMOS (heavily influential in New Labour's thinking), also expressed similar concerns and argued that the emphasis on qualifications in schooling should be reduced and that the skills needed for what he termed 'the new knowledge economy' should be integrated into mainstream teaching. Out of these concerns came the publication in 2003 of *Excellence and Enjoyment: A Strategy for Primary Schools* (DfES 2003). At its launch the then Secretary of State, Charles Clarke, said that targets would be dropped in 2004 in response to head teachers' complaints about excessive pressures and that there would be more autonomy for teachers in the way that they managed their classrooms. However, as Alexander (2004) has pointed out, the central dilemma of how teachers were to exercise this autonomy in a regime of targets and performance tables was left unclear. Although it has been argued that as teachers have grown in confidence their approach to literacy and numeracy has become more flexible (Ofsted 2002a), there is little sign from the reviews and surveys of teacher opinion, that work in primary school is less stressful as a result of these later initiatives (Galton and MacBeath 2002). Typical of the continuing dilemma facing head teachers in primary schools was the view taken by one of Ofsted's more recent Chief Inspectors, David Bell, who in his 2003 Annual Report (Ofsted 2004) argued that pressure on primary schools to improve literacy and numeracy was producing a two-tier curriculum while at the same time continuing to pressurise teachers by expressing concern that the test scores at Key Stage 2 were at a standstill.

Meanwhile the Standards Unit, under Professor Michael Barber, had employed a team led by Michael Fullan from the Ontario Institute to evaluate, at considerable expense, the implementation of the Literacy and Numeracy Strategies. Barber argued that this would ensure a different perspective and a detachment which would not be possible among

English researchers (Brehony 2005: 36). Three reports (Earl *et al.* 2000, 2001, 2003) were produced. Despite a long and distinguished publication record on school leadership in which Professor Fullan has argued for strong teacher communities which are highly intellectual as well as highly caring (Fullan 2001: 133), his evaluation team saw 'top-down, large-scale reform' as an interesting experiment and appeared to endorse the imposition of the Literacy and Numeracy Strategies on schools. Furthermore, the evaluation reports claimed these twin strategies had dramatically changed the ways that teachers thought about classroom practice. The evaluation team, however, were less forthcoming in estimating whether such changes in pedagogy had brought about improvements in pupils' learning. It was left to other British researchers, the ones whom Professor Barber had claimed were not able to bring sufficient detachment to the evaluation process, to undertake this assessment, as and when independent funding allowed.

Testing in the National Curriculum

When New Labour first set out as a national target that 80 per cent of 11-year-olds must reach the expected standard in English by 2002, the then Secretary of State, David Blunkett, promised to resign if this result was not achieved. By the end of 2001, however, it appeared that the upward trend in scores on the National Curriculum tests at Key Stage 2 had begun to reach a plateau, and this trend has been confirmed in recent years as Figures 2.1 and 2.2 demonstrate.

In English, girls reached their target in 2001 (80 per cent of girls gained Level 4 or better), dipped below in 2002 (79 per cent) but have increased slightly in each year until in 2005 when 84 per cent reached the target. For boys, however, it has been a different story. The gap between boys and girls has remained steady at around 10 per cent so that in 2001 the figure was 70 per cent while by 2005 it had reached 74 per cent. Consequently, overall only 79 per cent of Year 6 primary pupils have achieved Level 4 or better in English.

In mathematics less progress has been made, although the gap between boys' and girls' achievement is negligible as Figure 2.2 illustrates. By the 2005 tests, 76 per cent of boys had achieved Level 4 or above compared to 75 per cent of girls. The corresponding results for 2001 showed 71 per cent of boys and 70 per cent of girls reaching these levels. Thus in both cases the trend has been for the numbers of pupils reaching the required level to have risen between 1995 and 2000 and then to plateau.

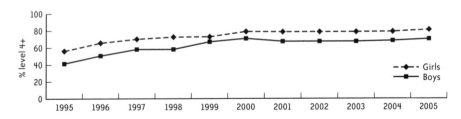

Figure **2.1** KS2 national curriculum results (English) 1995–2005
Source: DfES Annual Statistics Package

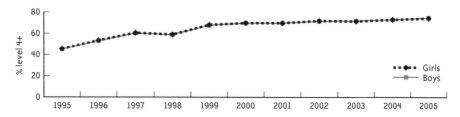

Figure **2.2** KS2 national curriculum results (Mathematics) 1995–2005
Source: DfES Annual Statistics Package

Earl *et al.* (2003) have put forward the view in their evaluation that some of these earlier gains may have been attributable to a 'Hawthorne effect', a phenomenon named after the researcher who was the first to suggest that any new innovation, however valid, brings about an initial gain in output because of the expectations surrounding the reform. However, Tymms and Coe (2003: 648) have also argued that the evidence for a massive rise in standards of literacy and numeracy, during the initial period of the strategy, is 'largely illusory'. Using their own specially constructed tests, Performance Indicators in Primary Schools (PIPS), data on reading and mathematics in over 100 schools was collected annually from 1995 (Tymms and Fitz-Gibbon 2001). The scores for reading showed little change, while in mathematics there were modest gains. Brown *et al.*'s (2003: 670) findings from a five-year study of mathematics (1997–2002) support those of Tymms and Fitz-Gibbon (2001) in concluding that there is little evidence that the national numeracy strategy has been an 'indisputable success as judged by a rise in attainment'. Brown and her colleagues, however, go further than other critics in suggesting that 'in some cases research evidence was disregarded for political reasons' because the government needed to justify the expenditure of over £400 million on implementing these twin strategies. Tymms (2004) is more charitable and attributes the improvement in scores mainly to changes in test construction.

Maximising a school's performance can be achieved in several ways. The first, as illustrated in the opening paragraphs in Chapter 1, relies on excessive coaching and the ability to teach children the various techniques required to score maximum marks on the test. In adopting this approach there is likely also to be an attempt to concentrate resources by dividing pupils into homogeneous ability groups. A second way of implementing such a policy is to provide 'booster' classes for pupils who need to catch up on their peers. Surveys have shown that this appears to be the preferred method adopted by most head teachers (Gray *et al.* 2003). In a telephone survey of 50 primary head teachers Gray found that the majority invested heavily in booster sessions with two-thirds operating this strategy from Year 3, although in a more limited fashion. However, his analysis of school data suggested that this was not always an effective policy. The assumption underlying the boosting strategy appeared to be that children should make steady progress in 'equal-sized steps' from year to year. If test performance on the intermediate optional tests did not improve in this way, then it was deduced that additional work was needed. However, Gray and his colleagues found that only a minority of pupils (39 per cent in English and 46 per cent in mathematics) conformed to this pattern. For some children progress occurred in increasing steps, for others it decreased and for yet others it went up and down from one year to the next. Yet these different pathways appeared to have only a minimal impact on the total progress which pupils made as they proceed through Key Stage 2. By far the greatest effect was the 'Year 6 push'. Gray and his colleagues concluded that there may be other more effective ways of improving performance than merely concentrating the main effort in Year 6. They suggest that schools should pay more attention to these different pathways to progress in the period before Year 6 in order to create 'more flexible and sustained approaches' which would ensure 'greater continuity for their pupils long before they encountered the demands of the Key Stage 2 assessments' (Gray *et al.* 2003: 42).

A third and less reputable way of improving test scores is to cheat. While in no way a justification for falsifying results, it is surely a measure of the pressure that some headteachers experience, which is caused not only by concern for their own standing, should their school be seen to be failing, but also by considerations on the effect that failure can have on some pupils. Cheating on the tests appears to have increased under New Labour according to Brehony (2005: 38), who cites the case of one headteacher who was jailed for three months for forgery (Woodward 2003). The same article alleged that the practice of cheating is probably more widespread than has been identified through prosecutions. According to Nichols and Berliner (2005), high stakes testing in the United States has resulted in nearly half of students in one Gallup Poll admitting that they cheated at least once on tests. In a review of press reports over a five-year period up to 2005, Nichols and Berliner identified over 60 major cases of fraudulent behaviour. In one case reported in the *New York Times,* 36 per cent of the schools in one down-town district were involved in passing crib sheets to students prior to going into the examination.

Nichols and Berliner (2005) point out that when the stakes are high the use of performance indicators inevitably leads to corruption. This is true not only of education but of business and other academic fields such as medicine. In their review these researchers cite numerous instances where in the pursuit of bonuses for high-performance company managers have found ways of manipulating the figures in order to maintain their increments.

Teachers and the primary curriculum

The net effect of New Labour reforms on primary teachers has been to increase their workload (Galton and MacBeath 2002). On average primary teachers now work between 52 and 55 hours a week and headteachers considerably more. The average teaching day has been extended and lasts 6 hours and 30 minutes (including break and lunch time) because many schools now tend to start classes before nine o'clock and cut out the 15–20 minute afternoon break. It appears therefore that the introduction of the literacy and numeracy hours have driven schools to increase teaching time in their attempts to maintain a broad and balanced curriculum. Much of lunchtime is also taken up with curricular activities under the guise of clubs and other optional events, in an attempt to compensate for subjects that are squeezed in the official timetable. Consequently there is little time left in the school day for

prospect of gaining success but of avoiding failure. This in turn offers a different perspective on motivation. The pupil's behaviour when faced with a challenging task is not only a function of the personality, expressed in terms of basic drives, but is also influenced by the manner in which pupils cope with failure. If a pupil attributes failure to a lack of ability, he or she may react entirely differently from a peer who believes the result will be largely determined by the amount of effort required (Weiner 1992). Dweck (1986), who argues that the view the child takes about ability is crucial to motivation, has taken these ideas a step further. If ability is thought of as something fixed, then the likelihood is that pupils holding this view will feel that they can do little to alter the course of events when faced with a task that they believe is too difficult for them. Only pupils with a strong belief in their own competence will be highly motivated. Others with little confidence in their innate ability are likely to display a response known as 'learned helplessness'. In contrast, pupils who accept that through increased effort previous failures can be overcome will concentrate on mastery of the task rather than concern of where they stand in relation to their peers (Dweck and Leggett 1988). Clearly one of the factors which influence these decisions is the culture in which the learning is situated. As Watkins (2003) argues, the current strong emphasis on performance in schools with their standard assessment tasks, league tables, target setting and so on all militate against a mastery orientation and reinforce those factors which give rise to strategies of task avoidance and teacher dependence resulting from fear of failure. Such behaviour may be further reinforced in anxious pupils (Covington 1992). There are also those who worry that demonstrating cleverness in class may have negative consequences for their standing within their peer group (Marsh 1989).

This somewhat extended discussion is necessary in seeking an explanation for the finding that while pupil motivation remained high, attitudes to the core subjects and to enjoyment of school fell over the course of several primary school years. The items in the motivation test inventory attempted to measure, in part, the intrinsic–extrinsic motivation dichotomy and were drawn from Entwistle *et al.* (1979) and Harter (1981). Other items were linked to the notion of achievement mastery (gaining success through effort rather than an innate ability) and performance (gaining satisfaction from doing better than one's peers) and were taken from Marsh (1989) and Coopersmith (1967).

In the analysis of the results from the transfer studies (Galton *et al.* 2003) and contrary to the theory proposed by Dweck, there was little distinction between those pupils scoring high on achievement and performance and those on achievement mastery. The tests were also given to the same pupils after their transfer to Year 7 with similar results, but on this occasion the opportunity to interview them about their questionnaire responses was taken up. It appeared that the pupils were no longer interpreting items relating to academic satisfaction or achievement performance in the competitive sense that they could out-perform their peers. Instead their main concern was to attain the required *level* of performance:

'I need to get Level 5 if I am to get into the top set.'

Other pupils were very clear as to the reasons for their motivation. Having said that much of the work they did in Year 7 was very like that carried out in Year 6, they responded to the interviewer's query of why they work so hard by replying:

'Because we need our education. We need to get good grades to get a good job and to get GCSEs.'

In a similar manner, achievement mastery was not so much about working hard in order to understand something intrinsically interesting, but stemmed from the satisfaction that came when meeting the criteria and fitting it in to the work in ways which gained the required level. So, for example, when Mrs Clarke informed children in Chapter 1 that they should introduce two more adjectives into their description or include some reported speech in the introductory paragraph of their story in order to gain an extra level, the pupils' motivation was directed towards finding ways of doing this without having to alter the overall theme of the writing. Consequently, pupils who score highly on the *academic performance* scale also tend to do as well on the *achievement mastery* scale.

However, although motivation, defined in this way, remained strong, there were negative consequences. By focusing on the required level and the techniques needed to achieve success, pupils tended to view any other demands which were superfluous to this goal as irrelevant to their needs. In particular, teachers have commented on the reluctance of more able pupils to do more work on a topic once the required level was achieved. In support of this view, pupils responded very poorly to an item on the motivation questionnaire such as:

'I try to learn as much as I can.'

However, they strongly agreed with items of the type:

'I learn just what I have to know to pass.'

'Outside school I am not interested in any of the subjects.'

Thus the emphasis on targets, levels, testing has not reduced the tendency for children in primary schools to engage with their tasks. What it does appear to have done is to have reduced and limited their horizons to merely doing what they need to do in order to succeed in gaining the required levels. In this sense Watkins' (2003) strictures about the negative effects of the current performance culture appear to be corroborated.

Changes in classroom organisation and classroom practice

One of the key innovations of the National Literacy Strategy was the implementation of the three-part lesson in which the majority of the session was to be spent in whole-class teaching. The Numeracy Strategy also emphasised a whole-class approach coupled with the use of 'interactive' teaching. This latter concept poses problems in definition since, as Robin Alexander argues, it is associated in the strategies with 'an officially promulgated view that lessons should maintain a good pace and be characterised by a sense of urgency driven by the need to make progress and succeed' (2005: 21). Alexander quotes Kyriacou and Golding's (2004) evidence that whole-class teaching with pace makes it difficult for the pupils to have sufficient thinking time in order to come up with reflective answers to the teacher's questions. He complains quite rightly that many of those involved in the strategy do not do what researchers seek to do; namely to separate the organisational component of whole-class teaching from the nature of the discourse that takes place during whole-class sessions (Alexander 2005: 21).

Indeed, many of the claims that the National Literacy and Numeracy Strategies have brought about fundamental changes in pedagogy are in reality references to changes in organisational practice rather than to the nature of the interactions taking place during classroom talk. Both the official evaluation (Earl *et al.* 2003) and Ofsted (2002b, 2002c) claim that major shifts in classroom practice have occurred based on their observations that there was more whole-class teaching, increased pace in lessons and greater attention to objectives rather than activities when planning lessons. These conclusions are endorsed in a more recent review by Webb and Vulliamy (2006) for the Association of Teachers and Lecturers (ATL). These researchers report that over 94 per cent of the lessons that they observed involved whole-class teaching compared to 50 per cent 10 years previously. They argue that the National Literacy Strategy has brought about profound changes, 'Not only in the primary teacher's classroom practices but also in their values concerning desirable practice' (Webb and Vulliamy 2006: 109). In support of this view they point to the work of Hargreaves *et al.*'s (2003) research on the impact of the National Literacy Strategy. Hargreaves and colleagues found that at Key Stage 2 there was a large increase in the number of questions that teachers asked children so that the overall ratio of teachers' questions to statements in comparison to earlier research (Galton *et al.* 1980, 1999) was very different. Hargreaves and colleagues concluded, however, that the teaching which took place during the literacy hour was only interactive in a surface sense because the initial questions really extended pupils in ways that required them to provide a sustained interaction in which they elaborated their initial answers.

While it would therefore appear that because of the shift to whole-class teaching more questions are asked in the course of a lesson, the key issue in determining the degree to which classroom practice has changed has less to do with the overall *quantity* of any given interaction and more to do with the *proportionality*, since the latter reflects the overall pattern of the exchanges between teachers and pupils. Figure 2.4 therefore examines five studies where classroom observations have allowed the patterns of questioning to be analysed. The first of these took place in classrooms during the late 1970s (Galton *et al.* 1980). The second was the replication of that earlier study in 1996 (Galton *et al.* 1999). In both of these studies systematic observation was used, whereby the researchers took with them into the classroom a set of pre-specified categories of teacher behaviours and noted which of these occurred every 25 seconds. In the third study (Hardman *et al.* 2003), video-recordings collected in 2001 were subsequently analysed. The fourth study conducted in 2002 again used systematic observation (Hargreaves *et al.* 2003), while the final set of data comes from the yet unpublished transfer study referred to earlier in this chapter.

The data in the figure displays a remarkable consistency across nearly three decades. In the original ORACLE study (Galton *et al.* 1980) the ratio of open to closed questions was 21.5 per cent to 78.5 per cent. Thus primary teachers, at a time when it was alleged that 'they told children nothing but left them to find things out for themselves', asked nearly five times as many closed questions requiring a specific answer as they did more challenging, open questions where more than one answer was acceptable. The replication of this study in 1996, marking

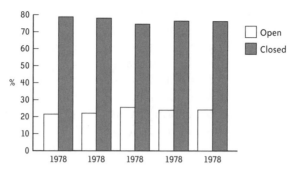

Figure **2.4** Open v closed questions
Source: Galton *et al.* (1999)

the end of the Conservative government's management of education, changed this situation by a relatively small amount (ratio of open to closed questions = 22.2 per cent to 77.8 per cent). By 2001 when New Labour's reforms were fully established the proportion of open questions had increased by around three and a half percentage points (Hardman *et al.* 2003) so that the ratio of open to closed questions was 25.6 per cent to 74.5 per cent. However, when Hargreaves *et al.* (2003) carried out their observations one year later, the ratio had fallen back to nearer the original ORACLE figures (23.9 per cent open to 76.1 per cent closed). The final set of data, collected in 2005 during the present as yet unpublished transfer study, arrives at a ratio of 24.2 percent to 75.8 per cent in favour of closed questions. These differences collected by different observers using varying methodologies and observation instruments are well within the bounds of experimental error, amounting as they do to variations of around 1.5 per cent from the overall mean. It would appear therefore that despite the pressures on teachers to engage in interactive teaching, little has changed in the course of nearly 30 years.

It is not possible to do a similar analysis on the various kinds of statements made by teachers because, unlike the use of open and closed questions, both Hardman *et al.* (2003) and Hargreaves *et al.* (2003) categorised statements in different ways from those used in the ORACLE research projects. In the ORACLE research task statements were coded as either *factual* or concerned with *ideas*. The remaining statements were either classified as giving *directions* about the task or as matters of *routine* (dealing with behaviour, giving instructions about where to sit, when to clear away, etc.). Table 2.2 sets out the percentage of different statements as observed in 1976, 1996 and 2005.

Table **2.2** The pattern of teachers' statements
Source: Galton *et al.* (1999) plus Galton's unpublished data

Statement category	Year of observation		
	1976	**1996**	**2005**
Facts	15.4	13.8	30.3
Ideas	5.6	9.4	8.4
Directions	52.0	45.8	47.1
Routine	27.0	31.0	14.2
Total	100.0	100.0	100.0

For both 1976 and 1996 the overall pattern is similar: most teacher talk consists of either giving directions about the task or in routine instructions. Statements concerning ideas are the least-used category, although there is some improvement over the two decades. But by 2005 the situation has changed. Although task directions continue to dominate the use of the fact and routine categories has been reversed. There is now less emphasis on routine instructions (14.2 per cent of all statements) and a doubling in the percentage of factual statements since 1976 (30.3 per cent compared to 15.4 per cent). It is possible to see this dramatic increase in the use of factual statements as a consequence of the increased pace of lessons coupled with a change in classroom seating arrangements as reported by Webb and Vulliamy (2006: 111). These researchers found that in 45 classrooms visited, 18 had the desks or tables arranged in rows and one in a horseshoe shape as suggested by Hastings *et al.* (1996). While, therefore, the patterns of questioning have remained stable, the shift to whole-class teaching seems to have promoted a dominance of teaching as *transmission* (Alexander 2004: 27). Similar conclusion are reached by Smith *et al.* (2004), whose analysis suggests that the rapid pace of teachers' questioning and the predictable sequence of teacher-led recitation in which the parts are nearly always being played out as a teacher–pupil–teacher interaction. Teacher-directed interrogation of pupils' knowledge and understanding was therefore the most common form of teacher–pupil interaction, with teacher questioning rarely going beyond recall and clarification of information. As a result teachers tend to 'exercise close control over the nature, pace and direction of the knowledge pursued in the lesson … the data suggests that the teaching was mainly interrogative and directive in nature' (Smith *et al.* 2004: 407).

There are some interesting conclusions to be drawn from the above analysis. In the workload study (Galton and MacBeath 2002) most teachers attributed their failure to change classroom practice to the constraints of the National Curriculum and its associated programme of testing. But the patterns of the analysis here suggests that while this may be true, in part, there are more deep-seated reasons for the sustainability of certain kinds of classroom practice, since the observations of teacher–pupil interaction go back to the 1970s in a period where there was considerable freedom for teachers to conduct lessons how and as they wished. To change classroom practice, therefore, one has to do more than simply change the patterns of organisation because, as Robin Alexander (2000) argues, classroom discourse is in large measure culturally determined. To change the way that teachers teach requires a shift in primary school culture, which can only come about if the principles governing the changes are clearly articulated and understood. This has not been the case with the promotion of interactive whole-class teaching as a core feature of the Literacy and Numeracy Strategies.

At its simplest, interactive teaching has often been contrasted with teaching as transmission, so that it represents a shift away from teachers *telling* to teachers *asking*. But as Alexander (2005: 21) comments, the guidance set out by those responsible for drafting the Literacy Strategy, that interactive lessons should 'maintain a good pace' and be 'driven by a sense of urgency', suggests that questions should be short, sharp and designed primarily to elicit either information or solutions to relatively simple, straightforward problems. More substantial questioning which encourages pupils to think through answers requires 'thinking time' and therefore requires a slower pace. What is not made clear, however, in all the advice offered is when teachers should use pacy questions and when to use more slow, more deliberative ones. This, it is assumed, is best left to the teacher to decide.

But as argued in the previous opening chapter, such decisions are the very stuff of what constitutes 'a science of teaching'. When to use one approach or another is surely dictated by the kind of learning that teachers wish to take place. While, therefore, a decision as to which kind of questions to ask is clearly related to the nature of the learning taking place, the manner in which those questions are asked must be left to the teacher who has unrivalled knowledge of the context governing this decision (the pupils' prior knowledge, current behaviour, the classroom environment, etc). Thus questioning might take place as a whole-class discussion with the teacher carefully scaffolding proceedings, or it might take place in groups or in a brainstorming session and so on. The literature on teaching methods (particularly that produce by government task forces, Ofsted, etc.) continually confuses the principles of teaching with the conditions necessary to put these principles into practice. The rest of the book, therefore, is an attempt to articulate some of these principles which can provide the framework for making choices in the matter of classroom pedagogy.

Evaluating New Labour's record

Before moving to the next chapter, however, it is perhaps useful to summarise briefly the main conclusions of this chapter on the state of current primary practice. Contrary to the official view, independent evaluations of academic progress suggest that New Labour has been less successful in raising standards than the government and its spokespersons have suggested. Gains, if any, have been limited to the first few years and have been accompanied by a serious deterioration in pupils' attitudes to school in general and to subjects such as English, mathematics and science in particular. Motivation appears to have changed in ways that do not encourage pupils to take up new challenges or to express themselves creatively. Teachers claim that they now work excessive hours in an attempt to deliver a broad curriculum and attribute their feelings of stress to the fact that the present government no longer seems to trust their judgements in curriculum matters. More seriously, primary classroom practice now seems more akin to stereotyped secondary school lessons, dominated by a fast pace, with restricted questioning and a tendency for teachers to control the discourse such that transmission rather than exploration dominates.

Even while publicly dismissing most of this evidence, the government has appeared to acknowledge the need to rethink its approach with the re-launch of the 2003 Primary Strategy *Excellence and Enjoyment*. The second half of the title, *Enjoyment*, would seem to recognise that there is an attitude problem (for both teachers and pupils) while continuing in the first part to perpetuate the view that:

> The Literacy and Numeracy Strategies have, according to all those who have evaluated them, been strikingly successful in improving the quality of teaching and raising standards in primary schools. (DfES 2003: para. 3.2)

And the document goes on to imply that the same methods should be extended to all parts of the primary curriculum. As Robin Alexander comments, however, the strategy is 'ambiguous to a point of dishonesty about the Government's intentions towards primary education' (2004: 28). He contends that despite the rhetoric of 'enjoyment' and 'enrichment' the strategy continues to foster a 'crude instrumentalism of purpose' which has characterised New Labour's time in office. Alexander directs some of his strongest criticisms to the document's section on learning in which he argues 'populist phrases seek to legitimate or disguise its impoverished thinking' (2004: 18–19). He deplores the fact that the strategy document has nothing to say on the processes of learning, and in particular the contrast between the view of the child as a 'lone scientist' as against a 'psycho-cultural account which emphasises the … social and interactive character of … learning' (2004: 18–19).

These strictures therefore provide both a warning and a challenge as we attempt in the next chapter to take up Alexander's challenge and to explore the nature of children's learning in an effort to make sense of different theories of the mind in ways that can accommodate the various goals of primary education.

Key references

Brehony, K. (2005) Primary schooling under New Labour, *Oxford Review of Education*, 31 (1): 29–46.

Hargreaves, L., Moyles, J., Merry, R., Patterson, F., Pell, A. and Esarte-Sarries, V. (2003) How do primary school teachers define and implement interactive teaching in the national literacy strategy in England?, *Research Papers in Education*, 18 (3): 217–36.

Webb, R. and Vulliamy, G. (2006) *Coming Full Circle? The Impact of New Labour's Education Policies on Primary School Teachers' Work*, London: Association of Teachers and Lecturers (ATL).

Chapter 3

Learning for Teaching

In the government's document, *Excellence and Enjoyment: A Strategy for Primary Schools* (DfES 2003) Chapter 4 begins with the comment 'every teacher knows that truly effective learning and teaching focuses on individual children, their strengths and the approaches which engage, motivate and inspire them.' And the authors of the document then go on to say that the new primary strategy will actually support greater tailoring of teaching to individuals. This view was further developed in the then Education Minister David Miliband's speech to the 2004 North of England Conference where he used the term *personalised* learning. According to the minister, this had to do with 'shaping teaching around the way that different youngsters learn' so that it nurtures 'the unique talents of every pupil'. The DfES on its website on personalised learning appears to wish to emphasise this uniqueness in that it sees the principle objective to be tailoring 'education to individual needs'. However, the view, as outlined in the first chapter is that pedagogy can only be developed if we start with the general principles concerning the way we as human beings learn before attempting, as Simon (1981) argues, to apply these principles to individual cases. In the same essay Simon points to the impossibility of devising a system based on 'individual needs', arguing that this would be akin to a small-group tutorial arrangement such as still exists in some universities and special schools. This would pose huge resource implications.

Charles Desforges, an ex-primary teacher and leading researcher on these matters, observes that schools would be even more successful in developing these principles that Simon called for over 20 years ago, if we could all learn to 'share and use the knowledge we have about learning'. Desforges accepts that there is a vast body of knowledge of learning which emerges from the everyday practice of teachers, but he observes that this knowledge is difficult to get at and therefore difficult to share. Thus we cannot base our ideas about pedagogy solely on 'craft knowledge'. But, and this is the concern of this chapter, he also observes that there is a small but strong body of scientific knowledge about learning to be gleaned from research. However, he argues that while this knowledge is easy to get, it is difficult to apply. He therefore suggests that the trick we need to perform is to bring the practical knowledge of teachers and the theoretical knowledge of researchers together in order to promote advanced teaching practices (Desforges 2003:14). In essence, Desforges is making a similar point to that made at the end of the first chapter concerning the need to use the principles of learning, developed from research and theory, and then to monitor the ways that teachers apply this theoretical knowledge so that it works in various classroom contexts.

One of the earliest attempts to link different theories of learning to particular teaching approaches was undertaken by Joyce and Weil (1972). These authors devote specific chapters to various interpretations of learning and then match these with transcripts of actual lessons in which teachers either deliberately or intuitively made use of these particular ideas. Joyce and Weil make the point at the outset of their book that attempts to compare one teaching method with another or to fashion one overall general teaching method (as in the case of New Labour's National Strategies) have a chequered history. Comparative studies generally show, these authors claim, 'that differences between different approaches are for specific objectives' and they go on to say that 'although the results are very difficult to interpret the evidence to date gives little encouragement to those who would hope that we have identified a single reliable multi-purpose teaching strategy as the best approach' (1972: 8).

Because researchers have developed a multitude of different ways of representing the processes that we describe as learning, Joyce and Weil begin by defining what they term a number of 'families of models'. Although different families are not mutually exclusive, they do represent distinct approaches to learning and teaching according to Joyce and Weil. There are, for example, models based on theories about information processing or behaviour, others which draw upon ideas about social interaction, and models which tend to emphasise the development of personal understanding and self-actualisation. However, the task of linking these families of models with a specific repertoire of teaching activities results in a series of networks that are extremely complex. For example, in the information processing category are listed seven alternative/complementary approaches, in the social interaction five, and in the personal models a further five. Recognising that such a degree of complexity was likely to limit the take-up of these ideas, a simpler version has more recently emerged (Joyce *et al.* 1997). However, it still remains a complex and rather formidable task for teachers to master the intricacies of all the different combinations. Since one of the arguments in favour of the models used by Joyce is that it is then possible to design a curriculum which reflects the 'learning styles' of different individuals, the task becomes almost impossible for a teacher faced with a class containing 30 or more pupils, and offends in part the principle which the late Brian Simon attempted to establish, namely that we should seek first to obtain general principles and then see how these principles can be applied to individuals in practice.

Ways of knowing

Galton (1995: 108) has argued that a more useful starting point, from a practitioner's point of view, might be to consider the kinds of knowledge demands which different tasks make upon the learner, and then to select an appropriate model of learning from the many, which seeks the inculcation, accumulation or development of this particular kind of knowledge. The starting point of this analysis is a simple three-part typology, which was constructed by Patricia Alexander and her colleagues, and was based on a synthesis of a number of articles in educational journals concerning the different ways that the authors wrote about knowledge when referring to learning (Alexander *et al.* 1991). These researchers argued that most knowledge acquisition involved either *procedural, conceptual* or *metacognitive* knowledge. Procedural knowledge is defined as more than 'knowing what' or the acquisition of new facts or new skills (usually called declarative knowledge). It also involves 'knowing how', that is, the ability not only to locate new information but also in which circumstances to make use of it (conditional knowledge). In today's primary classroom, where the use of the World Wide Web is fairly commonplace, the ability to locate information, restructure it for a particular purpose, and then to use it to illustrate a point or principle would encompass this kind of procedural knowledge.

Conceptual knowledge, Alexander *et al.*'s second over-arching category, concerns the knowledge of ideas, the way they function and the conditions in which they should be used. The term refers, by implication, to complex and often non-linear knowledge structures, unlike some simple mathematics or science concepts where the different parts constitute the definition of a whole (for example, simple fractions or states of matter). A key process in the acquisition of conceptual knowledge is the capacity to recognise instances of belonging and not belonging to a given class which defines the concept, as in the ability to understand what constitutes a mammal and what one does about creatures such as whales. Because there is often a potentially large number of characteristics which can be used to define any classification we often create sub-categories, which Alexander *et al.* term *domain* knowledge. Concepts which are central to a specialised field of study then become part of *discipline* knowledge. The final component of conceptual knowledge is the ability to convey these ideas to others. This involves knowledge about the use of appropriate language, *discourse* knowledge. Within the framework of a given discipline, it is also necessary to use a form of words that allows meaning to be conveyed as propositional statements. This has to be done in ways which make use of knowledge of the language registers that are appropriate for a given audience. Alexander *et al.* (1991) define knowledge of the available and relevant styles of spoken and written communication as *syntactic* and *rhetorical* knowledge respectively.

The third part of the typology, *metacognitive* knowledge, concerns the capacity to be aware of one's cognitive processes and an ability to regulate or manage this process unaided. According to Pintrich metacognitive knowledge involves 'knowledge about cognition in general as well as awareness of and knowledge about one's own cognition' (2002: 219). In recent years, the renewed interest by psychologists in this aspect of learning stems from the key part such knowledge plays in 'helping students become responsible for their own cognition and thinking'. Pintrich makes the point that this interest is common to most theoretical approaches to learning and development:

> From neo-Piagetian models, to Vygotskian and cultural or situated learning models, regardless of their theoretical perspectives researchers agree that with development students become more aware of their own thinking as well as more knowledgeable about cognition in general. Furthermore, as they act on this awareness they tend to learn better ... The labels for this general development tend to vary from theory to theory, but they include the development of metacognitive knowledge, metacognitive awareness, self-awareness, self-reflection and self-regulation. (Pintrich 2002: 219)

Metacognition also involves what Shulman (1986, 1987) has called *strategic* knowledge, or the ability to recognise what is an acceptable form of cognitive processing within a given domain or discipline and what does not conform to these rules. In science, for example, to test a given proposition we may need to design an experiment that controls for other interfering variables in the form of a fair test. Alexander *et al.* (1991) argue that beside strategic knowledge (that is, knowledge of appropriate and legitimate strategies) there must also be *self*-knowledge. This form of knowledge concerns the learner's capacity to regulate their cognitive processing and involves an ability to recognise errors and to monitor one's thinking. These various strands of the typology are presented in diagrammatic form in Figure 3.1 by way of a summary of Alexander *et al.'s* (1991) schema.

A framework for learning?

During this process of acquiring these three different types of knowledge there must be a shift in the way that information is processed. At the core of this transformation, according to Bereiter (1991), is a distinction between learning as an *additive* process and learning as *reorganisation*. This view is in some ways very similar to the model of learning put forward by Bennett *et al.* (1984) in their attempt to determine how well primary teachers matched tasks to their pupils' immediate needs. Among various categories these researchers distinguished between tasks that were designed to provide pupils with new knowledge in incremental steps and those that taught them to restructure existing knowledge so that problems could be examined in new ways or pupils could discover rules or ideas for themselves. Within Alexander *et al.'s* (1991) typology,

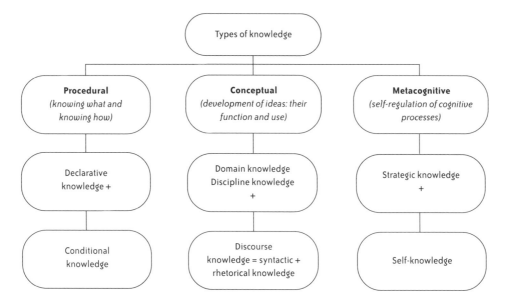

Figure **3.1** A typology of knowledge acquisition
Source: Adapted from Alexander *et al.* (1991)

which to a degree appears also to be a hierarchy, children move from a point where they acquire knowledge that is already known by others, to a point where they can order that knowledge within particular frameworks, to a further point where they can, without too much assistance, interrogate their own thought processes in creating their personal frameworks or restructuring existing ones. It is in this sense therefore that pupils eventually become 'metacognitively wise'.

Robin Alexander (2000: 344) is unhappy with some of Patricia Alexander's definitions. He criticises, in particular, the use of procedural knowledge as a 'catch all' term. He prefers to separate knowledge acquisition (*declarative* knowledge) from knowledge of routines, which can be defined as knowing where to gain such knowledge and how best to use it (*conditional* knowledge). One of the reasons why Robin Alexander is keen to separate the two is because his interest in classroom discourse leads him to emphasise the importance of Edwards and Mercer's (1987) distinction between *principled* and *ritual* knowledge. Edwards and Mercer point out that one purpose of teaching rules and relationships is to lead pupils to an understanding of certain principles (the way certain kinds of knowledge are organised), which belongs to the second of Patricia Alexander's typology categories of knowledge as *conceptualisation*. But learning a rule can also lead to merely repetitive performance in which the rules or procedures are memorised but cannot be applied in novel settings in a way that would support deeper understanding. Desforges (2003: 20) illustrates this by a story of a teacher who taught vocabulary by writing words and their definitions on the board and then getting the children to memorise everything that he had written. In the next lesson, as a practice/extension task, the class was asked to make up a sentence using the new vocabulary. One of the words on the list was 'stimulate' which the teacher had defined as to 'stir up'. One pupil wrote as her sentence, 'Mother stimulated the soup'.

As Robin Alexander (2000: 346) acknowledges, there is a case to be made for sometimes learning rules as a series of rituals and here he uses the obvious example of learning the 10-times table. One of the key differences noted by the author when sitting in Primary One classes in Hong Kong (6-year-olds) in comparison with UK classrooms is the extensive time taken over learning definitions and rules in the first years of formal schooling. In one classroom, for example, a whole 50-minute lesson was devoted to identifying the key characteristics which define rectangles. Children were encouraged to bring various empty packages (fruit juice cartons, washing powder boxes, etc.) from home, draw around the outlines and identify the rectangular shapes. The next lesson investigated the special case of the square, the next irregular rectangular shapes. In another class, the children played endless number games designed to create fluency in counting and manipulating numerals from one to ten. Hong Kong pupils top the international league tables in mathematics, yet from an English perspective these lessons appeared to 'over-teach' these topics. Similar examples can be found in Continental European countries. In Switzerland, for example, children entering the primary school after the age of six and a quarter spend much of the first year mastering the decimal number system in performing the four basic operations (addition, subtraction, etc.). The evidence suggests that this concentration on manipulating numbers, much of it through rapid oral question-and-answer sessions, pays off at secondary level where 14-year-old Swiss pupils were observed successfully completing tasks that are generally set for Year 11 in England (Bierhoff and Prais 1995).

There is, of course, as Robin Alexander (2000) points out, no way of knowing how an individual pupil perceives rules and procedures other than when he or she comes to use them. We know from the study of experts – and by definition experts must be metacognitively wise – that they have a principled understanding of rules, whereas the less competent performer generally has a ritualised one (Berliner 1994). Competent performers typically go through a recitation of the rules, and by a process of trial and error attempt to find the one which applies in a given case. Experts, on the other hand, seek to reconceptualise the problem in ways which allow them to identify the most appropriate rule to apply. The latter process is much faster and explains why Grand Masters at chess can take on and often beat the computer. Thus making the distinction between principled and ritualised knowledge, while useful in the analysis of discourse and for helping teachers to think about the way a task should be structured, doesn't in practice require changes in Patricia Alexander *et al.*'s (1991) typology provided, as is implied by these writers, that the three categories are viewed as part of a continuum. Because, for Patricia Alexander, the acquisition of declarative knowledge involving rules or routines is a means to an end (that end being to make pupils metacognitively wise) her main concerns are with principled rather than ritual knowledge. Further, from the point of view of developing an appropriate pedagogy for teaching rules and routines, it matters little whether the desired outcome is to promoting Bereiter's (1991) 'additive learning' (as with learning the 10-times table) or learning as 'reorganisation' (as with teaching vocabulary definitions of words such as 'stimulate' to use in sentences) since, as will be argued in this and the next chapter, the principles of instruction are much the same.

Learning as information processing

That being said, there seems a remarkable degree of agreement, as Desforges (2003) has claimed, concerning the implications for teaching what Patricia Alexander *et al.* (1991) term 'procedural knowledge'. At its simplest, learning can be conceived as a series of outcomes which result in an enduring change in knowledge or skill as a result from exposure to some experience. These outcomes are then committed to memory. Bredo (1997) has claimed that this kind of learning is underpinned by behaviourist theories, because it envisages that the knowledge to be acquired can be broken down into small steps and a degree of reinforcement can then be provided at various points along the way whenever success has been achieved. Such learning is also said to be *associationist* because one important technique for retaining this new knowledge in the memory is to build up chains whereby certain stimuli produce specific responses. Watkins (2003) describes this process as 'learning is being taught', or LBT for short.

More generally the kinds of processes used to acquire this form of learning can be encompassed within a general model known as 'information processing'. According to Meadows (1993: 213), the term is a collective noun for a series of explanations about how children use certain cognitive processes in order to process information that they acquire. The early theorists, such as Atkinson and Shiffrin (1968), suggested a parallel existed with computer hardware and computer software in their account of the memory system and distinguished between the memory structure, which is analogous to the computer hardware, and the manner in which the memory is controlled, which is analogous to the software. Successful learning therefore depends ultimately on the speed of operation and the memory capacity. According to the simple model, the mind, like a digital computer, has both short- and long-term memory stores and a central processing unit. The unit exercises executive control by utilising specific procedures and routines when solving particular problems. Many of these problems in computing are solved by a process of approximation and iteration. With the latter procedure, the first solution is arrived at by guesswork, perhaps on the basis of previous experience. This guess is then used for the initial calculation and the result fed back into the programme to provide a better solution. The result of this second calculation is again put back into the system and the process goes on till very little improvement can be detected in successive iterations. This process of successive iteration clearly has parallels with the view of thinking adopted by Bennett *et al.* (1984), which they termed 'restructuring and tuning'. Central to the theory is the idea of rehearsal (or practice) (Meadows 1993: 213), which enables information to be retained in the working memory (analogous to the central processor) for longer periods of time, and makes it more likely that it will be retained in the long-term memory store for subsequent retrieval.

Classroom studies by Alton-Lee and Nuthall (1992) and Nuthall (2000, 2004) have supported and developed these ideas regarding the function of the working memory. He and his research partner, Adrienne Alton-Lee, a former primary teacher, found that information that was relevant for successfully answering multiple-choice test items correctly was unlikely to be retained for more than two days, unless linked to other representations already in the working memory or which again entered the memory on the subsequent day. These researchers also found that pupils could generate simple constructs when there was an appropriate mix in the working memory consisting of a combination of specific information, generalisations, visual stimuli, word meanings and skills. In any one instance, the most effective combination depended on the task demand, so that a test question asking pupils to write down the temperature recorded on an accompanying picture of a thermometer was more likely to be answered correctly if the pupil had experience of carrying out the practical procedure of measuring temperature.

This brief account is a relatively simple presentation of the main ideas behind the information processing models of cognition, but nevertheless sufficient to meet the aim of establishing some general principles of teaching based on this working model of how pupils learn. As Meadows (1993: 223) argues, while the models work well for 'tasks which require conscious effort and strategic thought', they are less helpful in explaining tasks which children in the nursery appear to perform spontaneously (for example building a tower out of rectangular blocks). Perhaps more crucially in the search for suitable working theories of learning, information processing fails to account for what might be termed 'instantaneous restructuring', where one's ideas are transformed in a moment of inspiration rather than through the process of iteration discussed earlier.

Learning as constructing and reconstructing knowledge

This leads to the second possible working theory of learning based on the idea of *constructivism*. Whereas the computer analogy tends to see the take-up of information as a somewhat passive activity, at least initially, the constructivist approach regards the process as an interactive one. According to Piaget, for example, new information interacts with what we already know in two main ways. First, the new information is modified so that the brain can *assimilate* what we already know, and second, what we know already is modified to *accommodate* this new information. Thus in the earlier example of classification the pupil may well include a whale within the category of mammals because of similarities in the way its offspring are produced and reared, while ignoring the other characteristics that would associate it more closely with fish and other water creatures. Once, however, these latter characteristics are taken into account it becomes necessary for the pupil to modify the original conception of what constitutes a mammal, because of the *cognitive conflict* that arises when all the salient features of the whale are identified.

Conner describes this kind of learning as an active process of sense making. According to Conner, 'learning is determined by what goes on in children's heads and with how they make sense of the world. They do this by relating experience to existing organised concepts and principles which vary with each individual's past experience' (2003: 43). In this approach, the process of gaining new knowledge (or applying that new knowledge to different contexts) is seen as actively constructing and then reconstructing one's ideas. The process involves relating these new experiences to existing concepts, which in turn are conditioned by previous experience. Watkins (2003), taking a similar approach, also describes this kind of learning as individual sense making, or LIS for short. In contrast to LBT there is therefore no assumption at the outset that the learner is essentially a blank canvas or an empty container into which new knowledge must be programmed. Instead, the starting point is a belief that each individual has partial understanding of the world which he or she brings to every new experience. Thus in one lesson on evaporation for a class of 10-year-olds, the author placed a full glass of water onto a hot radiator at the start of the school day; by the afternoon some of the water had disappeared. To the question 'Where has the water gone?' the pupils offered a variety of answers among which were 'You drank it, sir!' 'The glass has got bigger' and 'Some of the water has escaped into the air'. In this situation, therefore, the teacher needs to find a starting point that takes account of individual pupil differences, unlike the simple information-processing model where a definition of evaporation would be presented to the class either verbally or more probably by means of a demonstration.

One metaphor which has been used to describe the role of the teacher within this constructivist framework is that of 'teacher as a gardener' since primary teachers are very fond of horticultural metaphors (Cortazzi 1991). Successful gardeners are skilled at planting seeds in suitable soil and aiding propagation by a combination of judicious watering and the application of fertiliser. In the same way teachers are seen to foster this process of construction and reconstruction by providing the necessary stimulating environment (soil conditions) offering well thought-out interventions (judicious watering) and engaging in supportive feedback by way of encouragement (fertiliser application).

Critics of the LIS model argue that an important defect is its lack of attention to cultural influences (Daniels 2001). If, the critics ask, the process simply involves an individual attempting to make sense of the surrounding world, why is it that the concepts that pupils with similar cultural backgrounds acquire have so much in common? For example, the notion of creativity in Western countries places a high value on the uniqueness of what is produced, whereas in Pacific Rim countries it places greater attention on striving for perfection. In one school visited by the author in Hong Kong, for example, the headteacher was a master calligrapher who enjoyed great esteem as an artist. His sole life's work as an artist consisted of repeated attempts to reproduce a perfect reproduction of the earliest manuscripts of the basic 1000 characters that constitute the main source of all written communication in the Chinese language.

Socio-cultural contexts in learning

The answer to the above concept, according to Bredo (1997), is that all learning is situated within a specific context. In this approach learning is seen as a form of apprenticeship whereby the learner engages in the process of cognitive development within a community as a way of gradually gaining acceptance as a full member of that community (Brown and Campione 1990; Lave and Wenger 1999). It extends the notion of reconstruction and construction but in a social context, so that the learner instead of being stimulated solely by the interaction with the environment now does so mainly by engaging in discourse with others who are more knowledgeable (Watkins 2003). For this reason it is often referred to as *social constructivism*. One of the best examples of this kind of learning occurs in the training of teachers. There would be few practitioners who would argue that they learnt more from their college courses than they did in working alongside their colleagues during teaching practice. Watkins (2003:14) terms this form of learning as 'building knowledge as part of doing things with others' (LBKO).

The theory that underpins learning as LBKO is derived mainly from the work of the Russian psychologist Vygotsky. At the heart of this theory, according to Wood (1998: 10), is the role of instruction in human development. One of the best known of Vygotsky's concepts is the *zone of proximal development* (ZPD), which he defined as 'the gap which exists for an individual child between what he is able to do alone and what he can achieve with help from one more knowledgeable or skilled than himself' (Wood 1998: 26). This leads to a different definition of *readiness* which Wood defines as 'the capacity to learn with help'. This contrasts with the position commonly attributed to Piaget, which conceives of readiness as largely dependent on an individual's current stage of development that varies from child to child. Robin Alexander takes a similar view to that of Wood, quoting Vygotsky's maxim that 'the only good teaching is that which outpaces development'. (2000: 425). He prefers a different translation of the ZPD which replaces the word *proximal* by either *next* or *potential*, because this emphasises the importance of teachers having high expectations when helping children through the zone (Alexander 2004: 11).

Watkins' (2003) distinction between LIS and LBKO is mirrored in the different ways that followers of Piaget and Vygotsky interpret the role of language in the development of the child's thinking. Wood, for example, argues that for Piaget 'language is a system of symbols for representing the world as distinct from actions and operations which form the process of reasoning' (1998: 25–6). He goes on to acknowledge, however, that:

> Piaget's position is more subtle than this statement suggests. Although language does not create the structure of thinking, it does facilitate its *emergence*. He [Piaget] suggests that it is through talking to others, particularly other children, that child's thinking becomes socialised. … But it is the structure of the child's intelligence, based upon activity, that determines when such collaborative exchanges come about. (Wood 1998: 28)

Thus Vygotsky, while accepting Piaget's view that children do not think like adults, argues that childhood speech is not simply 'a personal egocentric affair' but that it operates 'first as a regulative communicative function then later as a "tool of thought", not only providing a "code" or a system for representing the world but also a means by which self regulation comes about' (Wood 1998: 29). Furthermore, 'language does not simply reflect or represent concepts already formed on a non-verbal level but structures and directs the processes of thinking and concept formation themselves' (Wood 1998: 31). Accepting this proposition allows Robin Alexander to challenge the popular view of the teacher's hands-off facilitating role:

> The new approach demands both pupil engagement and teacher intervention. And the principle means by which pupils actively engage and teachers constructively intervene is through talk. (Alexander 2004: 12)

Others, however, such as Goswami (2001), claim that in the hands of his adherents Piaget's theories have undergone a radical overhaul during the last 20 years to be displaced increasingly by a more broadly knowledge-based view of cognitive development. Smith (1999: 150), for example, denies that Piaget neglected the socio-cultural dimension in learning and argues that those who seek to sharpen the contrast between Piaget's and Vygotsky's positions fail to distinguish between the former's attempts at dealing with a number of different epistemological questions. Smith argues that in his approach to constructivism Piaget attempted to address not only the psychological element dealing with the actual properties of reasoning in human minds, but also the different but equally important question of how such properties arise on the basis of 'naturalised activities in social worlds'. Critics, Smith contends, tend to focus only on the first question to the neglect of the second when considering Piaget's writings. Elsewhere, Smith translates from the original French text a detailed commentary by Piaget concerning Vygotsky's criticisms of Piaget's own writings on the language and thought of children to sustain the view that the differences between their respective positions are more apparent than real (Smith 1995). In translation Piaget agrees that all logical thought is socialised, 'because it implies the possibility of communication between individuals.' However, according to Piaget, there is a psychological dimension to this communication, since by definition any exchange between more than one person must of necessity involve 'communicative content' with one or more operation/s carried out by the respective individuals. For Piaget, therefore:

such interpersonal exchange proceeds through correspondences, unions, intersections and reciprocities, which are still operations. Thus there is an identity between these inter-individual operations. The conclusion to draw is therefore that operational structures which are spontaneously constructed during the course of intellectual development are in essence the structures of action coordination. Such coordinations are prior to the actions of individuals or to coordination between the actions of different individuals, and so to cooperation. (Smith 1995: 334)

More importantly, in the search for simple but useful working models of learning that can be used to fashion certain principles of teaching, Smith (1999: 159) notes that most viewpoints (whether individual or socially constructivist) would agree to the following propositions:

1. Construction is undertaken by learners not teachers.

2. Learners' constructions make use of available beliefs and expectations in grappling for new ones.

3. Teaching can provide the opportunity for, not the guarantee of, even the transmission of knowledge.

4. Construction always involves socio-cultural construction.

Shayer (1997) agrees that for the purpose of devising an effective strategy of intervention in the classroom, as a means of promoting *cognitive acceleration* in pupils, it makes little sense to distinguish between these different constructivist approaches. Brown and Palincsar (1986: 34–5) also argue that it is a mistake to see Piaget's ideas about child development in direct opposition to those of Vygotsky. They suggest that the two theories are different ends of a continuum and in support of this view they represent the process of learning as 'theory change'. Some changes can be brought about by supportive (social) interaction, while others can arise out of a situation where new experience conflicts with our existing knowledge producing the necessary degree of cognitive conflict. In a nice and apt description they make the point that at one extreme, that of the social interactionist, we hold conversations with others, whereas at the other extreme of the continuum, that of the lone scientist, we have similar conversations with ourselves. The essential point, however, is that the nature of the discourse is the same or similar in both cases (Brown and Campione 1994). Thus in seeking to create a simple working model of learning as a process of construction and reconstruction it seems that there is much to be said for combining Watkins' (2003) two categories, 'learning as individual sense making' (LIS) and 'learning through building knowledge as part of doing things with others' (LBKO).

Learning as developing expertise

When talking about learning, particularly when referring to ways that demonstrate their pupils' increased understanding, teachers use a variety of descriptions (Entwistle and Smith

2002). They talk about pupils 'internalising knowledge and skills', 'working out the rules or patterns', 'making concrete versus abstract representations' and 'organising ideas and reasoning'. Primary teachers, however, more often talk about pupils as 'independent learners' or 'independent thinkers', and this seems to imply something more than the ability to argue with oneself as suggested by Brown and Palincsar (1986). Patricia Alexander (2004: 10) contends that the study of expertise (and by definition experts must be independent thinkers) in the academic context is a neglected area of research. She argues that the acquisition of knowledge is a core objective for education and that a key aspect in this process is the ways in which individuals move away from a reliance on others for the acquisition of knowledge to a process where they can 'discover it for themselves'. However, the research into expertise which took place in the 1970s and 1980s was primarily dominated by the notion of 'artificial intelligence'. The researchers sought to determine the characteristics of expert problem solvers so that these features could be programmed into 'intelligent machines' or used to train non-experts. This has limited the application of this research to school settings, partly because in the work on artificial intelligence most attention has been paid to differences between novices and experts and not with the process by which one makes the journey from one extreme to another. Alexander (2004: 12) argues that since students will rarely leave school at 18 as experts in any subject domain, it is the process of transformation into experts through the stages of *acclimation*, *competence* and *proficiency* that is most relevant to teachers. At the acclimation stage, pupils begin to grasp the elements of *strategic knowledge* (Shulman 1986) which help constitute a domain (the forms of legitimate knowledge, what counts as evidence, ways of establishing the validity of a proposition etc). But because these pupils lack the ability to distinguish between accurate and inaccurate (or relevant and tangential) information, they are hampered in their thinking which therefore operates at a surface level. At the competence stage pupils' domain knowledge is more comprehensive and principled and a mixture of surface and deep-level strategies is used. The final transformation towards proficiency and expertise is marked by a shift away from these 'surface level' thinking strategies towards those which are of a 'deep processing kind' and a capacity to engage in *problem finding* as well as problem solving.

This stress on the importance of situating the development of expertise within the different knowledge domains recognises that academic disciplines are at the centre of formal schooling and that any working theory needs to relate to this 'unique socio-cultural context' (Sternberg 2003). However, cognitive processes by which this expert knowledge is acquired and gradually honed are common and concern what in her earlier writing Patricia Alexander *et al.* (1991) defined as 'metacognitive knowledge'. To become an independent thinker requires an individual to have knowledge of their own cognitive processes. There are two essential parts to this knowledge, one which concerns the development of a repertoire of strategies that can be used when confronted with a problem, and the other which consists of control mechanism that can decide which strategies are likely to lead to success and which to failure. In scientific hypothesising, for example, Alexander *et al.* (1991) argue that there is a need to develop mechanisms for evaluating different guesses, predicting the best solutions and for developing ways of testing these predictions.

It follows from the previous paragraphs that there is a specific role for teachers in helping children to become 'metacognitively wise'. Indeed, Robin Alexander has suggested that one of the key problems that can arise in primary schools when teachers seek to turn children into independent thinkers is the adoption of the maxim that 'we mustn't teach, we must let them learn' (1995: 31). Alexander objects strongly to this position:

> Underlying this [is a] simple confusion of teaching with telling which can be readily sorted out. Once this is done there is a genuine pedagogical issue – the degree of the teacher's mediation in the child's learning. I use mediation as the most neutral term available but of course the linguistic minefield here is a pretty extensive one and many of the other words of common currency carry strong adverse loading – direction, intervention, pushing, interfering, forcing, intruding. The competing imperatives therefore are clear and acute. While ideology dictates a teacher's role of facilitator and encourager, common sense (not to mention recent classroom research) indicates the benefit for children of powerful interventions by teachers, especially the kind which generate cognitive challenge. (1995: 31)

There are some researchers who, while agreeing with Alexander's proposition that it is important for teachers to present their pupils with situations which challenge existing thinking frameworks, would by inference suggest that the teacher's role in developing expertise is limited. This is because they view experts as people who are *born* and not *made*. Thus both Gardner (1995) in respect to art and music and Noice and Noice (1997) with regard to acting consider natural inherited talent to be the main determinant of expert performance. Both these writers argue that talent is a key to determining the final level of accomplishment and also in developing and sustaining interest. However, there are others who contest this proposition, notably Ericsson who suggests that 'much of the popular evidence for talent and explicable creativity is based on accounts that cannot be subjected to scientific analysis' (1996: 43). In support of the proposition that expert performers can be studied as 'an empirical phenomenon', he cites numerous studies from various domains such as athletics, chess and music to argue that motivation to practise for extended periods and a capacity to acquire from experience the ability 'to circumvent some basic information-processing limits' by enhanced 'anticipation based on predictive advanced cues' is the key determinant (Ericsson 1996: 43). In applying the discussion to the development of expertise in teaching, Berliner (2002) takes up a position similar to Ericsson. He points out that even those like Howard Gardner who place greater emphasis on the role of talent still recognise the necessity for deliberative practice in developing expertise. Thus it is likely, Berliner argues, that the context and deliberative practice are more important than personal characteristics. Berliner cites in support of this view the fact that expert ice hockey players and their coaches each separately listed the desire to become an expert (motivation) followed by good coaching and practice as the main determinants of success. Talent was only rated sixth of the 12 nominated factors.

Glaser (1987, 1990, 1996) argues that about two dozen propositions about expertise are defensible. Among these are:

1. Expertise is specific to domains. This concurs with Patricia Alexander's (2004) proposition that rather than teaching children generalised skills it is important to teach them to think as scientists, historians, creative writers, etc. Even where generalised skills are taught (for example, concept mapping) it is important to use these in different subject domains so as to ensure transfer from one domain to another.

2. Expertise does not develop linearly. At certain times plateaux occur that indicate shifts in the child's understanding and the stabilisation of certain automatic procedures.

3. Experts structure knowledge more effectively and represent problems in qualitatively different ways to non-expert thinkers. In general their representations are both deeper and richer and they are able to recognise meaningful patterns much faster than others.

4. Experts are also able to impose meaning when confronted by different stimuli. As such they are to be regarded as 'top-down processors' whereas non-experts are often misled by the ambiguity imposed by different stimuli and are likely to be bottom-up processors. Experts develop *automaticity* in their behaviour to allow conscious processing of more complex information. They also develop self-regulatory processes (or executive control) as they engage in these activities.

These propositions are derived from scores of studies in different fields ranging from chess to radiology and physics problem solving. They are supported by the work of Berliner (1994) in the training of teachers and by Bransford *et al.* (1999) in their studies of learning in schools.

The role of intuition in developing expertise

Unfortunately, from the point of view of those like Patricia Alexander (2004) who argue that children can be taught to become experts, the experts themselves are often unable to explain the rationale behind their decision making. They therefore find it difficult to pass on their ideas to experienced but less competent colleagues. Thus in a study of expertise in clinical nursing, Benner (1984) observed one experienced practitioner perform a lifesaving procedure in an emergency which none of her colleagues had thought of attempting. When asked why she acted as she did, the nurse expert replied, 'It just felt the right thing to do'. Such actions appear to be intuitive in the sense that the mind seems able to 'perceive the truth of the matter' without the need for reasoning or analysis. Indeed, Claxton (2000: 40) regards expertise as but one facet of intuitive reasoning which he defines as a 'family of ways of knowing'. Expertise, 'the unreflective execution of skilled performance', along with other elements such as implicit learning, sensitivity, creativity, judgement and rumination (or reflection on personal experience) makes up this family. Nevertheless, Claxton believes it is possible to 'learn to improve the frequency, reliability and quality of our intuitions', although he has little to say on how this should be done, apart from suggesting the importance of a cooperative, convivial and non-judgemental environment in which time is not of the essence (Claxton 2000: 48).

For Atkinson (2000) the distinction between expertise and intuition has more to do with thinking at a *strategic* and *tactical* level. Taking his example from teaching, Atkinson argues that while reasoning based upon theoretical insights may determine the planning stage of a lesson, once in the classroom the moment-by-moment decisions rely mainly on intuition, which is a product of experience. When this is coupled with a review of the lesson, then this process of reflective thinking allows the practical experience to be evaluated in ways that build into 'local, contextual craft knowledge' which then supports future planning. Atkinson's conclusion, not so different from that of Alexander *et al.* (1991), is that 'experience' (the opportunity to put strategies into practice) and 'feedback' (examination of how things worked out and how they might be improved upon in future) 'are key elements in developing competence and, eventually, expertise' (Atkinson 2000: 70). In the search for principles of teaching which help to make pupils 'metacognitivley wise' it may be of lesser importance whether we regard expertise as a facet of intuition or as the 'first impression' that helps to limit the range of possible strategies to be considered by the expert when starting to tackle a problem, as suggested by Bruner and Clinchy (1972). What does seem to be generally accepted on both sides of the argument is Claxton's (2000: 48) emphasis on a supportive environment. As Bereiter and Scardamalia (1993) observe, the conditions which foster the necessary motivational and affective dispositions appear to be crucial in explaining why some individuals persevere in their attempt to become experts while others succumb to the pressures involved. Watkins (2003) takes a similar position in arguing that the current *performance*-orientated environment in today's English primary schools (dominated as they are by league tables and national testing) is de-motivating, and the evidence presented in the previous chapter that showed dips in attitudes and a decline in mastery-orientated forms of motivation would support this conclusion.

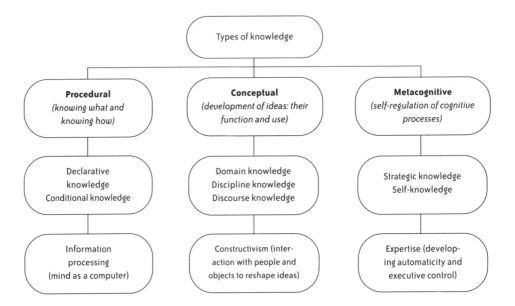

Figure **3.2** How pupils think and learn: working models

Thus to conclude, it has been possible to develop a framework for establishing key principles of teaching based on three working cognitive processing models of how children think and learn. This is shown in diagram form in Figure 3.2. The first of these models concerns the acquisition of what has been termed 'procedural' knowledge and derives its theoretical basis from information processing theory. In its simplest form this model views the mind as analogous to a computer. The second model of cognitive processing attempts to explain how human beings build and develop complex generalisations and rules. It is based on the idea that the pupils' understanding of the world in which they live comes about though a process of constructing and reconstructing previously acquired knowledge, either as a result of fresh experiences or through conversations with others who interpret this body of knowledge in different ways. Thus constructivism in the sense used here attempts to integrate both Piagetian and Vygotskian interpretations. The third and final strand concerns the capacity to think independently of others and is based on an understanding of the ways in which individuals in any particular domain acquire their expertise and how these expert performers differ from their experienced but less proficient colleagues. In the sense used here expert performance involves all those factors highly prized by teachers such as creativity, the capacity to solve complex problems and to undertake exploratory investigations. Its key components are the development of *automaticity*, whereby when faced with a problem experts can intuitively identify suitable strategies for finding a solution, and *executive control* that allows the expert quickly to determine which of these strategies are likely to lead to success.

Following this analysis, the next chapter will explore the principles of teaching that result from each of the three strands of the proposed working model in Figure 3.2 so that, to use Robin Alexander's (1995: 31) words, 'the nature of the teacher's mediation in the child's learning' within these various strands can be determined.

Seeking validation for the learning framework

There are, of course, other theories of learning which could have been adopted as part of this working model. One obvious weakness in the present selection is the lack of any reference to the affective domain, particularly the issue of whether certain forms of motivation encourage certain kinds of learning and if so, how teachers create a suitable classroom climate in which to foster these desirable traits. It was suggested in the previous chapter that there has been a significant change in the way that today's pupils are motivated to learn. The factors which spur pupils to work hard are now largely instrumental, to do with obtaining the necessary grades as a way of getting into a higher set in secondary school and ultimately good GCSEs, A-levels and a university place. For those not set on an academic career, it is the lure of getting a good job and earning money which is attractive. While such concerns have always featured in the ambitions of young adolescents, few of the early studies of vocational choice predicted that such considerations were a preoccupation of 10-year olds (Holland 1996). This and other issues will be explored in later chapters but a more pressing concern, initially, is to seek at least partial validation for the choice of the three working models of learning as a justification for putting forward some general principles for teaching in the primary classroom.

One alternative approach to the study of children's learning is through the classification of various 'teachable, partially proceduralised, mental activities' (Smith 2002: 663). The teaching of *thinking skills*, to use the more familiar term, has been widely used in post-16 education and is the subject of a detailed review by Moseley *et al.* (2005) for the Learning and Skills Development Agency (LSDA). These researchers note the growth in influence of these ideas in the 1980s with the development of various packages designed to teach basic skills in literacy and numeracy to children with special learning needs (Ainscow and Tweddle 1984). Interestingly, the same researchers also list the growth of interest in pupils' metacognitive processes as the catalyst for the renewal of interest in 'skill-based' approaches to learning. This interest has been stimulated in the United Kingdom as a result of a review by McGuinness (1999) that recommended more use should be made of methods designed to improve pupils' capacity to process information and to reason, enquire, create and evaluate.

Moseley *et al.* (2005) identified 55 different thinking-skill frameworks, of which 29 had been designed by psychologists, 21 by educators and 5 by philosophers. Three-quarters of these frameworks were created in the United States. In devising a model to accommodate the various thinking-skill approaches, Moseley and colleagues favour a three-pronged approach. This overlaps considerably with the framework developed earlier in this chapter from Patricia Alexander *et al.'s* (1991) categorisation of types of knowledge. Figure 3.3 presents Moseley *et al.'s* (2005) classification.

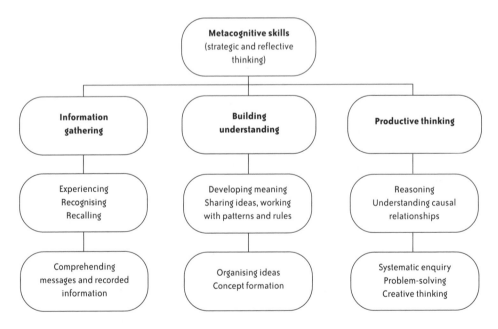

Figure **3.3** A classification of thinking skills
Source: Moseley et al. (2005)

The first of Moseley et al.'s (2005) strands is labelled 'information gathering'. It is mainly concerned with the acquisition of declarative knowledge, which is a component of what Patricia Alexander lists as procedural knowledge. Information gathering involves experiencing, recognising and recalling as well as developing the skill of comprehending and recording information. Missing from Moseley and colleagues' definition is the process of reorganising information (conditional knowledge), which appears to be viewed as a higher order skill. This seems a weakness, since Nuthall's (2000) research, mentioned earlier, clearly shows that the latter skill is a crucial part of information processing. One explanation may be that many of these skill-based frameworks identified by Moseley and his colleagues were developed in the early 1980s before the widespread use of the World Wide Web began to place more emphasis on the manipulation and re-ordering of information.

The second strand, labelled 'building understanding', includes concept formation and organising ideas and mirrors closely Alexander et al.'s (1991) category of conceptual knowledge. Within this strand the sub-category 'sharing ideas' makes a gesture towards the socio-cultural dimension of learning which is so strongly represented by the work of Vygotsky, although the overall emphasis within the strand tends to correspond to Watkins' (2003) LIS rather than LBKO.

The third strand, 'productive thinking', lists a specific number of cognitive skills that all require higher order thinking. Moseley et al. (2005: 378), however, wish to treat the metacognitive and self-regulatory processes as an over-arching function, arguing that despite the ambiguity and overlap in the definition of these terms (Zeidner et al. 2000) they can be applied to each strand of their model and essentially distinguish 'good' from ordinary thinking. In this they differ from Alexander et al. (1991), who appear to regard the growth of strategic knowledge and self-regulation as the final phase of a hierarchical development in learning to think independently of others. In part this can be explained because, while Moseley et al. (2005) follow Hacker (1998) in regarding metacognition as a conscious and deliberative process of thinking about one's thinking, Patricia Alexander (2004) tends to regard *automaticity* as the final goal insofar that the process becomes, to a degree, intuitive and *improvisational*, thereby allowing experts to think in fundamentally different ways from less advanced peers.

As will emerge in the subsequent chapters, this difference can be important in terms of how we set about teaching qualities such as creative thinking, systematic enquiry, problem solving and so forth, which are all listed in Moseley et al.'s (2005) third strand. For the moment, however, it is sufficient to note the considerable overlap in the categorisation used in both frameworks. Irrespective of how the twin processes of strategic thinking and self-regulation are employed, both skill-based and developmental approaches view these constructs as crucial elements in 'representing how people think and learn' (Moseley et al. 2005: 379). This provides a measure of confidence in seeking to move to the next stage of this analysis in which the implications for teaching are explored.

Key references

Daniels, H. (2001) *Vygotsky and Pedagogy*, Abingdon: RoutledgeFalmer. Chapters 1 and 2, pp. 1–68.

Meadows, S. (1993) *The Child as a Thinker. The Development and Acquisition of Cognition in Childhood*, Abingdon: Routledge. Chapter 4, pp. 197–251.

Watkins, C. (2003) *Learning: A Sense-maker's Guide*, London: Association of Teachers and Lecturers (ATL).

Wood, P. (1998) *How Children Think and Learn* 2nd edn, Oxford: Blackwells. Introduction and Chapters 1, 2, 3 and 4, pp. 1–109.

Chapter 4

Teaching for Transmission and Understanding

In the previous chapter different ways of looking at the process of learning were explored. The first approach was to regard learning as a change in the cognitive state of an individual which was not simply the result of maturation. The analogy used to represent this change was that the mind operated in similar ways to a computer so that learning was a form of information processing. The second approach viewed learning as a series of interactions between an individual and the surrounding universe. Whenever an individual faced a situation where exposure to new knowledge conflicted with what he or she already knew, then both what was new and what was already known underwent a process of construction and reconstruction. This state of *'cognitive conflict'* could be induced through exposure of the senses to various stimuli, but most importantly through conversations with 'others more knowledgeable than ourselves'. This process involves what Brophy (2004: 294) calls 'thoughtful discourse'.

These two views of learning lead to different models of pedagogy, the one which supports the notion of transmission of knowledge and the other which supports the application of that knowledge in ways that demonstrate understanding (Good and Brophy 2002). Furthermore, rather than contrast these two approaches in ways that forced earlier generations of teachers to polarise their choice of pedagogy between formal and informal teaching, as discussed in the first chapter, it makes more sense to regard the two approaches as being complementary. In support of this view, Good and Brophy argue that without the necessarily procedural knowledge and skills, pupils will find it difficult to engage in the kind of higher order cognitive activity out of which understanding develops. MacBeath and McGlynn (2002) also support this view in published research which attempted to provide a snapshot of the pupil's state of mind during the course of a lesson. The checklist was completed anonymously so that the teacher is unable to identify individual pupil responses. In one modified version of the checklist, for example, the present author has presented pupils with a series of statements such as:

- I am happy.

- I am bored.

- I am concentrating.

- I am anxious.

- I am wishing I was elsewhere.

- I am sleepy.

- I find time goes quickly.

At different times throughout the lesson each member of the class was required to tick the statements which best described how they were feeling using 'smiley faces' to represent a 3-point scale. Whenever pupils possessed the necessary procedural skills to cope with the more challenging tasks, they were observed to be totally engaged and seeming to derive energy and satisfaction from their work. On the other hand, where pupils did not possess the necessary skills for the task considerable anxiety could be generated. In such cases some pupils feigned a state of *learned helplessness*, claiming to know nothing and not to understand what they were being asked to do. In response to this self-induced dependency, teachers moved rapidly from being facilitators to instructors. At the other extreme, when pupils possessed the necessarily skills but were faced with a task which involved little challenge, boredom tended to set in. Whereas when the task neither provided challenge nor required use of recently acquired skills or procedural knowledge, pupils tended to become apathetic.

MacBeath and Glynn's (2002) statements have been developed from the earlier work of Mihaly Csikszentmihalyi (1990), who has put forward a view that whenever human beings come face to face with a challenging situation then a state described as '*flow*' can develop, provided the individuals concerned have the necessary skills to meet the challenge. Flow is said to be 'a powerful feeling of being at one with what you are doing, thoroughly engaged and deriving energy and satisfaction.' It is often seen at its most concentrated in sport where performers regularly set themselves targets above their present level of skill in order to improve performance (Csikszentmihalyi 1975: 38–48).

According to Csikszentmihalyi, a situation provokes anxiety when there is a high challenge but the person possesses a low level of skill to meet it, although an optimum level of anxiety can sometimes help the person to cross over into flow. When a person does have the necessary skill but is presented with something which does not offer a sufficient challenge, they can become bored. And when they are neither challenged nor require a great deal of skill to perform the task they experience apathy, as is indicated in Figure 4.1.

Csikszentmihalyi's use of the term 'skill' is very similar to Alexander *et al.*'s (1991) definition of procedural knowledge because it involves not only the acquisition of necessary information but also the rules for acquisition and the ways in which new information can be used. Acquisition of these procedural skills therefore differs from what is generally

	High challenge	Low challenge
High skill	FLOW	BOREDOM
Low skill	ANXIETY	APATHY

Figure **4.1** The concept of flow

meant by the term 'understanding'. Unfortunately, as Howard Gardner and Boix-Mansilla observe, 'while most observers would endorse the goal of teaching for understanding there have been only scattered attempts to find what is meant by this phrase' (1994: 199). Leach and Moon (1999) suggest that teachers tend to regard attempts to teach for understanding as a means of engaging students, sustaining their interest in continuing enquiry and leading them to see larger connections. For Brophy:

> Students who learn content with understanding not only learn the content itself but appreciate the reasons for learning it and retain it in a form that makes it usable when needed. (2004: 40)

As used by here by Brophy, understanding is contrasted with the mastery of content by memorisation through drill and practice. It therefore encompasses the acquisition of skills and procedures in the first strand of Patricia Alexander et al.'s (1991) typology. For Gardner, however, the term appears to be restricted to the operation of higher-order cognitive processes beyond information processing since 'students exhibit understanding when they can invoke ideas flexibly and appropriately to carry our specific analyses, interpretations, or critiques – and especially to perform their understandings with respect to new material' (1999: 169) The idea of viewing understanding as *performance* is central to Gardner's position for two main reasons. The first of these stems from the 'common-sense' observation that although understanding must involve the 'assimilation and transformation of knowledge, from the perspective of the teacher and the learner the physical events which occur in the mind or brain are far from transparent and, strictly speaking, irrelevant to their educational missions' (Gardner 1999: 160). But the second equally important reason for requiring students to *perform their understanding* is that it challenges 'traditional ways of doing (or not doing) things' whereby the teacher is required to 'look beyond mastery of dictionary definitions or the recitation of textbook examples'. Gardner goes on to suggest that:

> Focusing on performance immediately marks an important shift: Instead of 'mastering content,' one thinks about the reasons why a particular content is being taught and how best to display one's comprehension of that content in a publicly accessible way. When students

> realise they will have to apply knowledge and demonstrate insights in a public form, they assume a more active stance vis-à-vis material, seeking to exercise their 'performance muscles' whenever possible. (Gardner 1999: 161)

However, as was seen when the topic of metacognition was discussed in the previous chapter, the capacity to solve problems or critique new material, while it does go some way to predicting growth in a pupil's understanding, is not an infallible guide to expert performance. This is because in many cases, such as crosswords, it is possible to solve problems by trial and error once one has an inkling (from past experience) of the compiler's strategies for setting clues. For this reason other psychologists argue that it is always necessary for pupils to demonstrate their complete understanding in an observable way by making their thinking visible to the audience. This involves verbalising the various strategies used to solve the problem and reflecting on the relative strength and weaknesses of each approach.

Entwistle and Smith (2002) suggest that it is important for teachers to distinguish between what they refer to as *target* and *personal* understanding. Target understanding is mainly interpreted from the teacher's perspective. Within any given discipline there are patterns and relationships which are common to the professional community as a whole. These so-called *public* understandings become the targets that teachers want their students to understand (Newton 2000). However, because school learning is always, in part, socially constructed, other experiences that pupils bring to the classroom will dictate the extent to which their understanding of what is required of them by the teacher matches the teacher's expectation. These *personal* understandings therefore derive from the influence of significant others outside school, such as parents and peer groups. They are also affected by initial ability, prior knowledge, learning preferences and the student's overall dispositions for learning. Teaching for understanding therefore aims to present these target understandings in ways that take account of the personal orientations within the class so that the gap between what teachers hope the pupils will be able to do and the pupil's perceptions of what the teacher requires them to do is kept to a minimum. The idea that there may be a gap between what is in the mind of the teacher, when seeking to develop a pupil's understanding of concepts, and the minds of the pupils, when interpreting the teacher's goals, clearly fits with the constructivist view of learning. This follows from the discussion in the previous chapter where it was argued that conceptual learning was a process of transformation through continual construction and reconstruction. Once, therefore, it is accepted that there is a place for both knowledge transmission in order to facilitate the process of knowledge reconstruction, two questions then remain. First, is it desirable for the teacher to aim at one rather than the other, and second, what kind of pedagogy is best suited for bringing about two different but complementary goals?

Teaching as transmission

As we saw in the previous chapter, a number of researchers have been interested in the various ways in which the human mind processes information. Some of the ideas involving information processing have developed by using the analogy of the mind as a digital computer with its central processing unit, its short-term working memory and its long-term storage facility. The human short-term memory is very limited in the number of chunks of information it can hold at any one time. Our success in transferring it to our long-term memory store in a way which allows us to retrieve it from time to time depends on our ability to use certain routines. These routines enable us to encode the information and provide opportunities for repeated rehearsal of these procedures.

It has been shown that only about 40 per cent of material presented in an hour-long lecture is remembered immediately afterwards. After one week this drops to around 17 per cent, unless we take steps to slow down the rate of loss. Although in the first years of primary school, children tend to use repetition as the main way of retaining information, other more effective strategies (which do more than retain the information in the short-term memory for a few extra seconds) begin to develop by the time children have moved to Key Stage 2. Visual imagery, by conjuring up a link between words and objects, appears to be particularly effective because it 'transforms or elaborates' on new information, 'thus enriching it and linking it to what we know already' (Merry 1997: 51).

More pertinent to the teaching of primary school pupils is the work of the late Grahame Nuthall and his collaborator Adrienne Alton-Leigh, which was referred to in the previous chapter. These researchers spent time observing the teaching of certain New Zealand curriculum units in a number of schools. Pupils were pre-tested and then tested immediately after the class session, as soon as the unit had ended. They were then again tested and interviewed 12 months after the unit was originally taught to see how much of it they had remembered. Thus these researchers were able to distinguish between knowledge that was already known before the unit was taught and knowledge that was acquired as a result of the teaching (incorrect answer on pre-test but correct answer on post-test). In a similar fashion the researchers could also determine what was not learnt during the unit (incorrect answers on both pre- and post-test) and what knowledge was retained over time (correct on both the immediate post-test and again 12 months later). As discussed in the previous chapter, Nuthall and Alton-Leigh (1993) found that, typically, item-relevant information or experiences would be retained in the student's working memory for no longer than two days, unless it could attach itself to other bits of item-relevant information that was already in the working memory or that had been retrieved from long-term memory during that or the subsequent day. This suggests that a crucial element of the particular pedagogy required when teaching for transmission will concern itself not only with the introduction of new knowledge (the analogy is with the initial programming of a computer), but also with the repeated use of that knowledge either in the form of homework or by recapitulation at the start of the next lesson. For long-term retention, these researchers suggest that a number of strategies tend to be particularly valuable, and these are shown in Figure 4.2.

Clearly, as we move down the categories from *obtaining information* to *evaluating the consistency, coherence* and *verifiability of information* in Table 4.1, the distinction between teaching for transmission and teaching for understanding becomes somewhat blurred. Indeed, Alton-Lee and Nuthall (1998) include a fifth category, *achieving metacognitive awareness*, which has been omitted from the figure but will be discussed in the next chapter. This inability to maintain a rigid demarcation between the acquisition of procedural and

Table **4.1** Instructional processes for facilitating student learning

Learning process	Facilitating instructional approach
1. Obtaining information	Demonstrations
	Field experiences
	Brainstorms
	Teacher–student discussions
	Teacher explanations
	Student interaction with digrammatic representations, visual resources, textual resources, artefacts, Internet
	Informants' narratives
	Dialogue
	Use of teacher–student questions to focus on what pupils know already/don't know/need to know
	Identifying process for students to find answers to questions they don't know or need to know
2. Creating associative links	All the above but particularly:
	Brainstorming
	Teacher–student discussions of related student experiences and knowledge
	Visual, textual, enacted representations/interpretations by students
	Peer interaction (in pairs or groups)
3. Elaborating content	Teacher–student discussions (for example, instances/non-instances)
	Individual/group task engagement
	Visual, textual, enacted representations/interpretations by students
	Peer interaction (in pairs or groups)
4. Evaluating the consistency, coherence and verifiability of information	Creating an evaluative climate in the class which gives priority to critical thinking
	Teacher modelling of this evaluation process
	Facilitating argument/debate among peers
	Use of peer checking routines

Source: Adapted from Alton-Lee and Nuthall (1998)

conceptual knowledge arises because in certain cases generalisations and constructs can be generated when there are a sufficient number of representations in the working memory (in much the way that the computer lumps bits of relevant information together to create sub-routines). If this were not true then those of us whose schooling consisted almost entirely of rote learning would have been at a severe disadvantage in later life. Alton-Lee and Nuthall (1998) give an example of this process from data collected in a class of New Zealand 9-year-old pupils who were studying the topic 'Weather: observations and forecasting'. One of the pupils, Rata, was unable to define the symbol for a cold front on the pre-test. The lesson began with the teacher handing out two weather maps taken from the local newspaper. The maps had the symbols for cold and hot fronts in the legend beneath them. The following exchanges then took place:

Teaching for understanding

Desforges' assertion (backed by a wealth of research evidence) that direct instruction is best used for knowledge transmission and is less effective when deeper understanding is required, is also reflected in Alton-Lee and Nuthall's (1998) distinction between the generation of specific knowledge constructs and more generalised generic schema. They argue, for example, that specific constructs such as 'What causes rain?' or 'What is an anticyclone?' are inevitably linked to larger generic schemas about the nature of the physical world. In one example, when a pupil was asked to describe why she thought it was colder at night she replied:

> Because when it was cold people might want to have warm clothes and that people on the other side of the world would like a time when they had the sun so that it was much better to sleep when it was dark. (Alton-Lee and Nuthall 1998: 46)

In constructing this response it is clear that the pupil lacked a general schema which included knowledge that the sun is a source of heat and that the earth goes round the sun. Furthermore, she also lacked the metacognitive knowledge to be able to recognise that her argument or explanation was inadequate. Understanding involves the application of procedural knowledge in the development of these generic schema or concepts. As discussed at the beginning of the chapter, the process by which conceptual understanding develops, as interpreted by those who espouse constructivist models of learning, requires the teacher to create a classroom in which 'thoughtful discourse' (Brophy (2004: 294) regularly occurs as a means of helping pupils to reconstruct and transform their ideas.

Brophy (1992) has reviewed various programmes designed to teach understanding across a range of subject disciplines. He notes that in attempting to create a suitable classroom climate in which thoughtful discourse can take place these programmes have a number of common features. First, and most important, content is organised around a limited set of powerful ideas in a way that engages students' interests (Roth 2002). For example, in a science lesson on sources of energy the teacher first introduced the topic to a class of 10-year-old pupils with reference to global warming and its consequences. Second, the pupils' knowledge about the topic is explored and used as the starting point for instruction. In the above example the teacher asked pupils to think about various sources of energy and how they were converted to other forms. This was done by showing pictures of various objects on an overhead projector (a torch, a solar panel on the roof of a house, a car, a wind turbine, etc). Third, the pupils' initial ideas are then challenged by allowing them to explore the phenomena in question. Whenever possible this is done through direct, hands-on experience rather than by the use of texts or through teacher's narrative descriptions. In the above lesson pupils were provided with a number of simple experiments involving a magnifying glass (to heat paper), tuning forks (which were struck and placed on a tightly stretched string) and batteries and bulbs. Following the practical work, the class discussed whether their initial ideas about energy needed to be modified in the light of their experiments.

The consequences on pupil motivation when content is not organised around a set of meaningful ideas is illustrated by the following exchange between the teacher and a pupil. The lesson consisted of completing a series of mathematical puzzles in the form of magic number squares (a simplified form of *Sudoku*). The following exchange took place when a pupil, named Ian, left his place and went up to the teacher's desk:

Ian:	Why are we doing this?
Teacher (somewhat aloof):	Because it's interesting.
Ian (very firmly):	No it's not.
Teacher (perhaps a little patronisingly):	Well, you may think differently one day. It may come in useful.
Ian:	Have you ever used a magic number? In real life?
Teacher (more warily now):	No.
Ian (somewhat triumphantly):	Well! If you tell me what it's used for in real life I'll do it, but if it's not of any use I'm not interested in doing anything with it.

Source: Galton (unpublished)

Cultivating thoughtful discourse

As reported in Brophy (2004), one researcher (Newman 1992) conducted a survey of several thousand secondary students and asked them what motivated them to take part in class discussions. Like Ian in the above extract, most said that discussion worked best when the content of the lesson was *authentic* in the sense that they could link the ideas involved to their own everyday experience and not necessarily, as Ian appears to suggest, that there was a practical outcome. Newman (1990), in an earlier study, identified a number of features that characterise thoughtful discussion; the key ones are summarised below:

1. Students generate original and unconventional ideas through the use of open questions which allow a range of possible answers.

2. Students are given plenty of time to think before being required to answer questions.

3. The teacher presses students to explain and justify their assertions rather than accepting them or reinforcing them indiscriminately.

4. The teacher models the characteristics of 'thoughtful discourse' in his response to students by showing interest in their ideas and by 'thinking aloud' when engaged in problem solving.

The use of open questions has been a long-standing problem in teaching. In Chapter 2 it was shown that although the Literacy Strategy had promoted the greater use of questions,

In Chinese classrooms, according to Cortazzi and Jin (1996), classroom dialogue is teacher centred but organised for high-quality classroom interaction. Children are confident and speaking is fluent, although it generally follows the model laid down by the teacher (speak when one has something important to say). In Chinese thinking the notion of the individual has connotations with being self-centred and selfish. Cortazzi (1998: 210) speculates that a topic, 'People who help us', in an English classroom would translate into, 'People who help others' in a Chinese context. The importance of listening (to the teacher and other pupils) is stressed and it is not unusual for the teacher to ask another child to comment on a pupil's answer to a question, particularly when the first response is unsatisfactory, by asking 'Can you help Ka-ki, who doesn't understand?'. Cortazzi attributes the differences between this approach and that typically found in Western orientated classrooms to the value system derived from the 'longstanding Confucian heritage' which inculcates the belief that 'attainment depends largely on effort rather than ability', and stresses that teachers and pupils have 'mutual responsibilities and duties towards each other' (1998: 213).

The willingness of pupils to share their knowledge in this way is not a common feature of English classrooms. Cortazzi provides an interesting illustration of this cultural divide by recounting a conversation that he overheard at the school gate of an English primary school between a Chinese parent and her daughter. The child is being rebuked for talking too much but replies as follows:

Child: But my [*British*] teacher says we have to speak out, just give our own ideas and opinion. Just say what's on our mind.

Mother: I see you children in the playground, notice everyone talking. No one listening. Children may have opinions but they are no good unless they listen to others. Those British children are very conscious of themselves, but not of others. (1998: 213)

Biggs (1994) also attributes the willingness of pupils in Chinese classrooms to participate in classroom discussion to the nature of children's attributions when faced with difficulties with their learning. Whereas children in the West tend to attribute failure to learn to a lack of ability, those in the East are more likely to put their failure down to lack of effort. Hence there is more willingness to accept help from others, rather than regarding those who answer questions as 'boffs'. In English primary classrooms, at least initially, therefore, thinking time may be best achieved by asking children to discuss the questions with their neighbour or in small groups. In class discussion teachers should try to eliminate the kinds of responses identified by Alexander (2004), which lead pupils either to give short unelaborated answers or to attempt to remain silent by pretending that they are still thinking about a response. These include summarising, repeating or reformulating the pupil's answer or exhorting pupils to remember what was said or done earlier.

Explaining why as well as how

The third key element in teaching for understanding requires the teacher to encourage explanations and elaborations of answers. Here again from the analysis of classroom discourse in five cultures, Robin Alexander (2000) demonstrates that teachers are not good models in this respect. As illustrated in the extract of the teacher's exchange with the pupil, Ian, classroom practitioners rarely justify their decisions in class nor do they attempt to situate the learning in a wider context by telling pupils, as in another earlier example, how the conversion of energy from one form to another relates to global warming and the survival of the planet. In most Chinese classrooms, according to Cortazzi and Jin (1996), correct forms of speech are encouraged and a similar approach has been observed by the author in Hong Kong P1 (6-year-old pupils) classes when children are involved in group work. In some English language classes, for example, cue cards are provided on which words such as 'because' are printed and the class have a rule that any statement or suggestion must be followed by using one of the words on the cue cards to make a sentence.

Because it would appear alien to our present patterns of classroom discourse for pupils to explain or elaborate in response to teachers' questions, it is clearly necessary to offer training and to couple this with subsequent debriefing during which pupils have an opportunity to evaluate the quality of their responses. One example of this approach occurs in the work of King (1992), who made use of a strategy developed by Palincsar and Brown (1984) which they called *reciprocal teaching*. In this approach, originally designed to improve low-ability pupils' reading comprehension, students took turns to lead discussion on written texts. When reading any text students had to make use of a four-fold framework that required them to generate appropriate questions, summarise the content, clarify meanings and make predictions about what would happen in the next paragraph. In later studies the framework has been extended for use with other forms of material, such as graphical representations (Moore and Scevak 1995). Pupils in King's (1992) study were provided with generic question stems to guide discussion. Pupils were taught the different uses of *why*, *how* and *what* questions by learning, for example, to differentiate between a request to *explain why* and *explain what*. Pairs of pupils then practised giving explanations to different question stems. King (1992) found that during subsequent discussions pupils raised more critical thinking questions and provided more elaborated explanations when compared with a control group who did not receive any training.

There is also perhaps another reason why it is rare to observe teachers encourage pupils to elaborate their answers. This arises out of what appears to be an inbuilt mechanism among primary teachers, in particular, to provide, as far as possible, equal amounts of attention to all pupils. In the original ORACLE study (Galton *et al.* 1980), for example, the average amount of individual attention that a pupil received was very close to the maximum possible. Thus if there were 30 children in a class during the course of an hour's session, each pupil could, in theory, receive 2 minutes of the teacher's attention. Allowing for the time it took for the teacher to move from one child to another (often in very crowded classrooms that required the teacher to take a round-about route) the observed average of 1 minute 37 seconds was very close to this maximum. Furthermore, there were only small variations in the amounts of attention received by pupils of differing gender or ability. It was as if each teacher possessed an in-built clock that allowed him or her to devote more time to some pupils rather than others during the course of a particular lesson, or in the course of a particular day, but to correct this imbalance on the next available occasion. Teachers would often tell observers after a lesson that 'I spent extra time with Steven today because he missed out yesterday.' Although the shift to whole-class teaching since the introduction of the National Curriculum, together with the prescriptive literacy and numeracy hours and coupled with the increased use of classroom assistants will have decreased the amount of time a teacher spends with individual pupils, this principle of sharing out time equally would seem to be embedded in the culture of primary teaching. Encouraging children to elaborate their answers runs contrary to this *fair-share* principle because it is clear that not all children can be given the same amount of time during a class discussion, and the temptation will be for the teacher to pick the more articulate, able children in order to improve the quality of the discourse. A more clear-cut case is that of group work, where it is customary for teachers to ask each group to report back at the end of a lesson. If the teacher asks the first group not only to report what they did but to explain why they chose a particular way of tackling the task, then it puts additional pressure on the later groups when they come to report their findings. As a result, it is not unusual for teachers to preserve the first principle of *fair-shares*, by allowing each group a limited period in which to report on what they have done, with insufficient time for any further elaboration.

A teaching framework for developing understanding

In the section on teaching for transmission it was possible to produce a sequence of specific classroom practices (questioning, instruction, practice and so on) which combined to form a specific pedagogic approach known as *direct instruction*. It is now possible to do something similar in relation to teaching for understanding, although the descriptions are naturally more generalised because, as discussed in the first section of this chapter, to say that a pupil understands something implies a number of possibilities. Brophy (2004: 41) refers to the statements as key features which characterise the conditions for promoting understanding rather than indicating a set of sequential actions, as in the case of the direct instruction approach to teaching for transmission. In other words, if these features are not present it is unlikely that understanding will develop. Table 4.2 displays these key features.

Table **4.2** Ten key features in teaching for understanding

1.	Pupil exploration will usually precede formal presentation.
2.	Pupils' questions and comments often determine the focus of classroom discourse.
3.	High proportion of pupil talk, much of it occuring between pupils, so that the metaphor 'teacher as a listener' and 'guide on the side' rather than as a 'sage on the stage' are characteristic of the lesson.
4.	The lesson requires pupils to reflect critically on the procedures and methods used.

Table **4.2** (*continued*)

5.	Whenever possible, what is learned is related to the pupils' lives outside school.
6.	Pupils are encouraged to use a variety of means and media to communicate their ideas.
7.	Content to be taught is organised around a limited set of powerful ideas.
8.	Teachers structure tasks in ways which limit the complexity involved.
9.	Higher-order thinking is developed within the context of the curriculum and not taught as a discrete set of skills within a separate course unit.
10.	The classroom ethos encourages pupils to offer speculative answers to challenging questions without fearing failure

Source: Adapted from Brophy (1992)

The ten key features of the lesson which seeks to promote understanding relate closely to the theoretical principles outlined in the second half of this chapter. The first feature, indicating that exploration of the pupils' ideas should usually precede the teacher's formal presentation of new information, and the second concerning the use of these ideas to focus subsequent discussion, stems from the constructivist viewpoint that children are not empty vessels into which knowledge is poured. Thus even in the case of a most abstract concept the pupils are likely to have partial, if incorrect, understandings on which the teacher must build. The third proposition regarding pupil talk and 'teacher as a listener' contrasts with the balance of classroom talk during direct instruction. During the latter teaching approach, teachers dominate the exchanges in keeping with the well-known two-thirds rule initially postulated by Ned Flanders (1970) and confirmed by numerous other studies (Dunkin and Biddle 1974). The rule states that, typically, two-thirds of the class time is spent in talk and for two-thirds of that time it is the teacher who does the talking. The third key feature also implies that cooperative learning involving pair and group work will be a frequently used strategy. So far little has been said about this aspect of teaching, although research in primary classrooms over several decades still shows it to be a 'neglected art' (Galton 1981; Kutnick *et al.* 2002). The topic of groups will be considered in a subsequent chapter.

The fourth key feature is about developing 'metacognitive awareness' and marks the beginnings of the process where pupils learn to become independent thinkers. This is the third strand of Patricia Alexander *et al.*'s (1991) knowledge typology and forms the central theme of the next chapter. The fifth characteristic addresses the question of authenticity in support of the proposition that learning is more meaningful when it can be situated in contexts with which pupils can readily identify (Putnam and Borko 1997). The use of a variety of means and media to promote understanding (sixth key feature) stems from Howard Gardner's (1983) theory of multiple intelligences. Gardner argues on the basis of his theory that concepts can be well understood only if pupils can represent its core features in several ways. Thus it is desirable that multiple modes of representation draw on a number of intelligences. For Gardner this is not simply a case of ensuring that there are sufficient representations to cover different pupils' intellectual strengths, but more importantly to demonstrate the 'intricacy' of the subject matter:

This tack is more than a 'smørgasbord' approach to education – throw enough proverbial matter at students, and some of it will hit the mind or brain and stick. The theory of multiple intelligences provides an opportunity to transcend mere variation and selection. It is possible to examine a topic in detail, to determine *which* intelligences, *which* analogies and *which* examples are most likely to capture important aspects of the topic and to reach a significant number of students. (Gardner 1999: 176)

The seventh feature is related to the need for teachers to capture the pupils' interest, thereby, hopefully, motivating them to learn. But an added bonus in adopting this approach is that the learning can lead to a *transformative* experience, in that it does more than add to the store of the student's knowledge and 'enables him or her to see some aspect of the world in a new way' (Brophy 2004: 267). It follows from this that it is important, initially, to structure the task (eighth key feature) so that the student doesn't feel that it is too demanding. This process, which is termed 'scaffolding', will feature prominently in the next chapter.

The ninth key feature contrasts with current government policy which seeks to promote structured thinking skills programmes as part of the Personal, Social and Health Education (PSHE) and citizenship curriculum. The argument here concerns the well-known problem of 'transfer' of learning (Salomon and Perkins 1989) where students often find it problematic to apply the skills learned in one subject domain to another. On the other hand, as McGuinness (1999: 7–8) argues, when thinking skills are taught within subjects there is a danger that 'they may get lost in the midst of subject knowledge-based teaching and pupils may fail to see the connections between similar types of thinking in different subjects.' For this reason McGuinness suggests a compromise or 'middle way' whereby 'contexts are first identified within the curriculum where particular thinking skills can be developed.' Lessons are then developed where 'thinking skills and topic understanding are explicitly and simultaneously pursued.' This issue will be considered further in the final chapter.

The final key feature concerns the creating of classrooms as 'learning communities' (Watkins 2005). For Watkins such classrooms are incompatible with the contemporary accountability culture, which raises problems of implementation that will also be left to the final chapter. In learning communities, according to Watkins, pupils equate learning with effort and not ability, promote disciplined discourse and share responsibility for 'knowing what needs to be known and ensuring that others know what needs to be known' (Watkins 2005: 56). The result is that learning is richer and knowledge is co-constructed. To this end Watkins quotes a conversation with two 11-year-old pupils:

Even if you learn something perfectly or are a pioneer in your area, all your work is useless if nobody else can understand you. You might as well have done no work at all. The point of learning is to share it with others. Lone learning is not enough. (2005: 57)

This seems as good a point as any at which to leave the discussion of teaching for understanding and move to the third strand of our model for learning which deals with the acquisition of metacognitive knowledge. Here the goal is to enable pupils to think through problems with minimal support of the teacher by engaging in an internal dialogue within themselves. This then is the central theme of the next chapter.

Key references

Brophy, J. (2004) *Motivating Students to Learn* 2nd edn, Mahwah, NJ: Lawrence Erlbaum.

Edwards, D. and Mercer, N. (1987) *Common Knowledge: The Development of Understanding in the Classroom*, Abingdon: Routledge.

Gardner, H. (1999) *Intelligence Reframed: Multiple Intelligences for the 21st Century*, New York: Basic Books.

Chapter 5

Making Pupils
Metacognitively Wise

A third way of thinking about learning is to view it as a process of developing expertise. In setting out the implications that this working theory has for teaching in primary classrooms, it may be useful to begin with an illustration taken from the world of the theatre. There are of course links between acting and teaching in that many primary practitioners tend to put on a performance when in front of the class. Within primary schools, generally, there has also been a long-standing tradition of using creative artists and theatre in education groups to stimulate pupils' creativity. In its current form, such activities are supported through Creative Partnerships, sponsored by the Department of Culture, Media and Sport, which has invested millions of pounds in bringing what are now termed 'creative practitioners' into schools to work with teachers and pupils. This initiative has come about because it is generally recognised that these outside experts are able to motivate reluctant learners in ways that many teachers find difficult to emulate. On occasions these artists can also obtain outstanding work from pupils who previously have been regarded as 'problem children' by their teachers. One example, observed by the author, concerned pupils from a London primary school who worked with a video artist to produce a multi-media presentation of their family histories. This work was considered so outstanding that it was exhibited at the Photographers' Gallery in London's Leicester Square.

One particular illustration, however, does not concern school children, but a group of teenage dancers who were preparing for a professional West End show, the musical *Oklahoma*. Rehearsals took place in a large provincial theatre where there was to be a preliminary run of three weeks in order to iron out any problems. The show's director enjoyed an international reputation, in particular for working with amateur child actors and producing outstanding performances from them.

However, on this particular occasion teenage professional dancers had been hired to play the cowboys in the musical. The life of many professional dancers is in some ways like that of session musicians: in the course of a week they may go from one kind of job to another. On one or two days they may provide the chorus for a television show and on the next they may be involved in a commercial. However, the much sought-after jobs are those in the theatre, particularly when it involves a long-running West-end hit show. To progress in their careers, therefore, dancers need to be able to pick up new routines very quickly. In making a commercial, for example, where cost is a prime object, they are likely to have very little rehearsal time before the actual filming takes place. Dancers therefore need to be quick-witted and exhibit flexibility, but the conventional view is that they don't need to approach their tasks in an intellectual way. Over time, with experience, certain sequences of steps evolve into set routines, which suggest that coaching and practice through direct instruction is the most appropriate pedagogy. Dance routines are therefore taught mainly through the choreographer modelling the sequences and the dancers then engaging in intensive practice.

Imagine the surprise among the dancers, therefore, when on the first day of the three-week rehearsal period no choreographer turned up. Instead the director invited them to join with the actors, although usually the two don't tend to mix. On the first day the director began by showing the cast old cowboy films. During the subsequent days they were asked to read stories written by cowboys about their life on the range. They acted out scenes where they attempted to brand a steer, and they were taught to spin a rope and lasso an object. The group spent lots of time sitting in a darkened room discussing endlessly, or so it seemed to the dancers, the problems of loneliness that beset a cowboy on the range. During the course of the week the dancers became increasingly frustrated, insisting that they needed to get on and practise the routines, otherwise they would not be ready for the first night of the production. They argued with the director, telling him:

> We're not actors. We don't need all this background. Just block out the part of the set where you want us to be, get the music going and we will take it from there. If you don't want us to mess up on the first night you've got to give us time to practise.

It turned out, however, that their fears were totally unfounded. On the first night critics hailed the dancing as the outstanding part of the production. The dancers gave all the credit for this to the choreographer and to themselves, all of whom had worked long hours in the subsequent two weeks of rehearsal in order to make up for lost time. However, there was possibly another reason, and this had to do with the director's decision to make them spend the first week gaining experience of the way that cowboys lived and worked. By teaching them to understand what it *felt like* to be a cowboy he had empowered them *to dance like* a cowboy. In the same way, by teaching pupils to understand what it is to be a mathematician, scientist or historian children can come to think and act like mathematicians, scientists and historians. Psychologists refer to this kind of knowledge as *metacognition* or knowledge of one's cognitive processes (Bransford *et al.* 1999; Pintrich 2002). Without this type of knowledge it is impossible to regulate one's thought processes and engage in problem solving without help. By teaching children to think and act in this way they eventually become what Lahelma and Gordon (1997) call a 'professional learner'. This is particularly true at secondary level, where pupils have to cope with large numbers of teachers and more subjects. Evidence from follow-up studies of primary children at the end of Key Stage 4 suggests that if pupils transfer to secondary school without beginning to develop this kind of control over their own learning they will experience a considerable handicap (Sammons 1995; Sammons *et al.* 1993).

Anne Brown (1997) argues strongly that towards the end of the primary stage in particular, when children are beginning to learn how to regulate their own thinking in order to develop metacognitive capacities, one of the key roles of the teacher is to provide appropriate frameworks or scaffolds in which children can attempt to work things out for themselves. The idea of providing this kind of support appears to have been initially developed by Bruner (1966), and is analogous with the idea of providing a scaffold around a building when it is under construction in order to provide a safe environment for the workers. Many teachers operate this principle without really knowing that they are doing so. For example, a teacher might encourage pupils to improve their vocabulary by learning how to describe an object and might offer the pupils cue cards with words such as *colour*, *shape* and *size* printed upon each of them; in describing an object pupils are expected to say something about its colour, shape and size. At a later stage children who are writing their own stories might be asked to check five or six points concerning the description of characters, the presentation of the plot and so on. Critics of those who wish to scaffold every piece of learning argue that the teacher must avoid the danger of allowing the scaffold to become a prison so that, for example, children always describe objects only by their colour, shape and size. It is important therefore to scaffold in a flexible way that allows children to include their own creative thoughts. For example, the teacher who used the cue cards with colour, shape and size might have inserted a fourth card that said 'say what you find interesting about this object'. This allows for a degree of spontaneity. Webster *et al.* (1995) have used this notion of scaffolding in the context of the Literacy Curriculum. Included in the areas for which scaffolding seemed to be helpful were the tasks that enable children to extend conceptual understanding so as to make links with existing frameworks. For Webster *et al.* this involved creating frameworks for:

- locating and weighing evidence;
- marking critical features;
- looking for alternative ways of proceeding;
- assessing the need for additional support;
- taking stock and revisiting the nature of the task; and
- bridging: finding analogies, parallels and links.

Then at a later stage, when pupils are required to mediate their newly developed understanding through different forms of texts, the teacher needs to provide further support by way of:

- enabling pupils to find appropriate ways with words;
- creating thinking dialogues; and
- reviewing the process of learning and its outcomes.

Scaffolding in science lessons

Science seems to cause particular problems. Not only do attitudes to science dip sharply even in primary schools (Jarvis and Pell 2002), but observational studies (Cavendish *et al.* 1990) show that even when teaching the so-called *process skills* teacher talk tends to dominate. Several possibilities are put forward to explain this finding. First, there is the argument that teachers lack the necessary subject knowledge to conduct more open dialogue with their pupils, while others suggest that the pressure of getting through the curriculum forces teachers to cover the content matter at a fairly rapid pace. Others argue that having to teach to the National Curriculum tests, which by their nature tend to emphasise content rather than process, limits teachers' opportunities to engage in discussion.

However, Robin Alexander in an earlier study (Alexander *et al.* 1989) suggests that it is the failure to provide the necessary framework that may be the problem. He reported that some teachers were reluctant to encourage children to work in collaborative groups during the science lessons because they found that discussions often went off the point and they then had to intervene in order to 'get something done'. One teacher told Alexander, 'I don't see the point of wasting time in saying the same thing to five or six groups when I can say it to one large group as a class' (Alexander *et al.* 1989: 256–7).

Similarly, in a study of group work (Galton and Williamson 1992) a science lesson was observed whereby a class of Year 6 pupils were sent into their groups to brainstorm. The task was to find explanations of why, when they put their ear to the floor of the classroom, they could hear the vibration of traffic from outside. Having come up with their ideas they were then asked to devise some kind of test to see if their explanation was correct. The teacher reported that she had abandoned the activity and converted it to a class lesson because so much time was wasted in the groups by children arguing about impossible explanations that could not be subjected to a reasonable test. For example, one group had been arguing whether there was a tunnel beneath the ground and the traffic noise was being conducted along it. Their experimental test was to dig a hole under the floorboards. This teacher was clearly on the 'horns of a dilemma' concerning the point at which she needed to intervene; she did not want to stop the children thinking their own thoughts, but at the same time wanted those thoughts to be productive so that by the end of the lesson they would have carried out a fair test of their hypothesis.

In analysing the teacher's problem, we need to note that there was little attempt to provide the pupils with a suitable framework in which they could conduct their investigation so that they could learn to think like scientists. Experienced scientists in a similar situation – seeking to explain a phenomenon such as vibration – tend to do so within a clearly identified framework. For a start they will tend to reject any idea that they cannot test. Furthermore, they will tend to reduce, at least initially, the range of ideas even further to those that they can test with the conventional instrumentation that is available in the laboratory, since extra effort is required to design, develop and build a completely new apparatus. In setting out the brainstorming task this teacher might therefore have provided a scaffold in which the children were given the following set of instructions:

1. To collect everyone's ideas without at this stage commenting on any.

2. To sort the ideas into those which can be easily tested and those which can't (*in this way the idea of a tunnel below the floorboards would have been put into the reject pile*).

3. To reject any explanations which it was not possible to test with the apparatus available (*in this case, a set of tuning forks, different lengths of string and a means of clamping the string so that it remained taut*).

In this way it would have been possible to undertake the main point of the activity, that is, to devise a fair test in order to determine whether the pupils' explanations were valid ones, but to do so within a framework which restricted the number of choices. Note also, perhaps more importantly, pupils have been presented with one possible strategy for solving problems in science.

It now becomes possible to complete the third part of our framework relating different kinds of knowledge to various *working theories* concerning the ways that pupils learn, and to add the consequent teaching strategies that can be used to achieve these learning goals. In Figure 5.1 this is shown in diagrammatic form. The twin key elements in thinking metacognitively (that of selecting appropriate strategies and recognising the rightness or wrongness of the particular chosen strategy for solving a specific problem) demands that teachers scaffold not only the task itself but also the form of feedback given and the process of *debriefing* or evaluating the success or failure of the chosen strategy carried out. In this way pupils are helped to build up a *repertoire of strategies* that can be used to solve future problems.

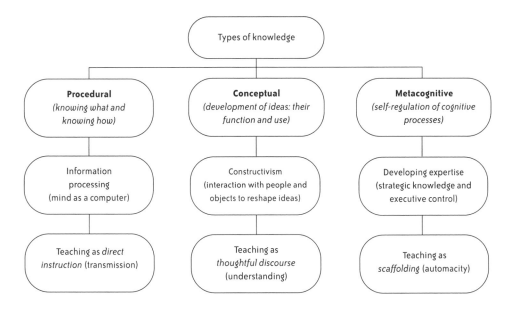

Figure **5.1** Knowledge, learning and pedagogy

Different forms of scaffolding

Rosenshine *et al.* (1996) have identified several different kinds of scaffold that are regularly used in teaching. The first of these consists of giving pupils *procedural prompts*. Rosenshine and his colleagues provide, by way of an example, one use of Brown and Palincsar's (1986) *reciprocal* teaching process where pupils were given a passage from a newspaper. This described the difficulties faced by children attending inner-city schools because of the prevalence of gangs largely based on racial groupings. The students were first asked to consider filling in the blanks in a number of questions to illustrate the different use of 'how' and 'what' questions. Thus to the stem '… gangs stop students from coming to school' pupils had to insert either the word, *how* or *what* and then discuss how the answers would differ in the kind of information provided. Rosenshine and colleagues argue, however, that there are limitations to the use of this approach because it can end up providing so much support that the students do little in the way of mental processing themselves. When this happens it is said to be the result of *over-prompting* and, as such, it does little to help students learn to generate their own questions.

The second form of frequently used scaffold involves modelling, where the teacher demonstrates the procedure and the students are then asked to generate something similar in another context. Modelling is often used in problem solving where the teacher thinks out loud, thus making their expertise explicit and available to the pupil. Another variation of the modelling procedure occurred in the topic where students were presented with the newspaper account about the difficulties of coping with gangs in inner-city schools. Students had to generate their own questions and then compare them with a set of model questions provided by the teacher. They then had to discuss among themselves whether the model questions were more effective.

Another alternative is to provide pupils with a list of possible *anticipated difficulties* that pupils are likely to experience when attempting to solve a particular problem. The teacher anticipates some of the common errors that the students might make during a particular task and discusses these before students attempt the activity. Thus in the earlier example involving Brown and Palincsar's (1986) reciprocal teaching approach in helping children to generate appropriate 'how' and 'what' questions, the students were given a list of inappropriate ones that they might be tempted to generate. Pupils were initially provided with a short written passage and then asked to decide whether or not a particular question from the list was concerned with the most important information in the paragraph. Pupils then subsequently went on to discuss why the question was a poor one, either because it was too narrow or too focused. In this way they were gradually taught to recognise good questions from poor ones.

The fourth type of scaffolding strategy is to *regulate the difficulty of the material* so that pupils move from relatively simple short examples to much longer complex ones. The fifth type of scaffold involves the use of *cue cards*. This was considered earlier in the chapter in the case where the teacher provided a framework for describing an object by referring to its colour, shape and size. However, by far the most frequently used scaffold in the primary classroom consisted of what Rosenshine *et al.* (1996) term *guided student practice*. This tends to be heavily teacher-directed, as in the earlier example where the teacher in the science

and II' because the tasks which define these categories mainly concern the acquisition of procedural knowledge as defined by Patricia Alexander *et al.* (1991) in the earlier chapters.

An example of a task which might carry with it high ambiguity but low risk would be one in which the class was placed in groups and asked to brainstorm on deciding the best way to survive if their vehicle broke down in the desert. Here there is great uncertainty about the correct answer but little risk to individuals because it is done in groups, and under the rules of brainstorming, no comments can be made when the initial suggestions are put forward. Doyle (1983) argues that most tasks where teachers seek an opinion rather than a definitive response can be classified under this heading.

Highly ambiguous and high-risk tasks are those where teachers seek to develop understanding so that pupils will, over time, become 'metacognitively wise'. By their nature such tasks are likely to be highly challenging, and several possible answers will be acceptable to the teacher since one of the learning goals is to evaluate the appropriateness of the different responses. In one case observed by the author, for example, pupils were asked to draw a picture about the 'Christmas story' without any further guidance as to what the picture might or might not contain. They were simply told that the best three would be chosen to represent the school in a local newspaper competition. Other activities in this category might involve imaginative story writing, designing an apparatus for measuring time using a variety of simple materials (string, sand, empty plastic bottles, etc) or consideration of certain moral or social questions.

Clearly, one purpose of scaffolding is to reduce the degree of risk and/or ambiguity. Examining the various scaffolds identified by Rosenshine *et al.* (1996), it can be seen that there are two ways in which they achieve their effects. One kind of scaffold reduces the ambiguity and therefore reduces the risk, while the other reduces the risk, while maintaining the ambiguity. Doyle (1983) argues that in most cases teachers tend to opt for the former strategy, but implies that when attempting to develop deeper conceptual understanding (and metacognition, although he doesn't use this term) it is more important to use the second approach and to attempt to lower the risk while maintaining as much ambiguity as possible within the task. Thus the most frequently used strategy, guided practice, is one that reduces ambiguity and therefore lowers the risk, as in the sequence described by Doyle and Carter (1983). There, pupils only begin to participate in the writing exercise once they have narrowed the range of possibilities through persistently questioning the teacher about what she had in mind. In general, it is the scaffolds that are derived from the cognitive development literature (cue cards, self evaluation and so on) which satisfy Doyle's criteria for promoting understanding, and not those emanating from the teacher-effectiveness research.

By way of illustration consider two lessons during a literacy hour session, where the learning goal is to develop the pupils' capacity to describe characters in their story writing. The subject of study concerns the mother of a family living in Trinidad whose home has been destroyed during a violent storm. While the father sits under a tree, consoling himself with a bottle of rum and bemoaning the family's fate, the mother busies herself creating a temporary shelter and sets the children to gathering materials for a fire, so that when the evening comes they can have warmth and hot food. Having reminded children of the story (read on the previous day), the author's revised field notes show that the first teacher continued as follows:

The teacher begins by asking the class to tell her something the mother did or said.

Sam: She made a tent.

Teacher: Good. What does that tell you about her? [pause] OK! When someone gets on and does things while others watch, what do they say they are?

Sam: Busy.

Teacher: OK! Yes, but I'm thinking of a better word beginning with the letter 'R'. Anyone help me?

Tina: Rushing.

Teacher: Yes, she was busy and she did rush about, but can anyone tell me what this word means? [*Writes the word 'resourceful' on the board; one pupil is asked to look it up in the dictionary.*]

Eventually the class go on to discuss things the mother said and establish (with much prompting by the teacher) that she wasn't cross with her husband because he wouldn't help. Under the heading DESCRIBING WORDS a picture is eventually built up on the board of a mother who is loving, kind, resourceful, tolerant, good organiser and so on, and in each case an example of something the mother said or did is included by way of illustration. The class are then set the task of writing a description of the mother using some of the describing words on the board but finding illustrative examples of their own from the story.

In the case of this first teacher, the task was scaffolded by a guided approach. She begins by going around the class asking questions about what the mother did or said, and also the part played by her character in the story. The children offered various suggestions which were then refined by the teacher's comments and written up on the board. The children were then told to write their descriptions using some of the words or phrases from the board, but the task was extended to promote understanding by getting pupils to choose their own illustrations from the book. In terms of Doyle's (1983) analysis set out in Figure 5.2, the ambiguity surrounding the task is considerably reduced and this also lowers the risk to the children. They are helped by the teacher to choose an appropriate sequence of words which say something about the mother's role in the story. There is far less risk to the task because as long as they use the words which have been approved by the teacher and are written on the board, then there is less chance that they will make an incorrect response. Thus the teacher has lowered the *risk* of pupils misunderstanding what they are required to do by lowering the *ambiguity* involved. The pupils were provided with a list of descriptors to use, and although the teacher, before they began writing, told the class they were free to substitute their own alternatives, few (if any) of the children took up this challenge.

The second teacher adopted a different approach, as the following account illustrates:

The teacher began by going over the main points of the story. She continued by asking the class to say what had impressed them about the mother's behaviour. The discussion was much more open-ended than in the previous example and children were generally asked if they would have behaved in the same way in a similar situation.

Teacher:	So she [*the mother*] didn't shout at him [*the father*] to come and help?
Karen:	No. She just let him go to sleep while she got on.
Teacher:	Would you have done the same?
Karen:	No. I'd have given him a big kick to wake him up and told him to come and help.
Teacher:	So what does that tell us about the mother?
Karen:	She's kind.
Stephanie:	She's patient
Steven:	She's frightened of him. He's drunk and he might hit her and she doesn't want the children to see.
Teacher:	That's interesting. Can you find anything in the story to support your idea? Something someone did, said? Anyone else [*to the class*] help Steven here?

The teacher continues the discussion in this way for several more minutes. None of these ideas are written down on the board. The teacher then tells the class they are to write a description of the mother using the following framework which is displayed on an OHP:

1. *Write five lines about what the mother did that tells you something about her.*

2. *Write five lines about what the mother said that tells you something about her.*

3. *Write five lines describing her habits (how she dressed, walked, spoke and so on).*

4. *Write five lines about the storyline and the part played by the mother in the action.*

5. *Write five lines about anything else you would like to say which tells you something about the mother's character.*

Here the teacher scaffolds the task by reducing the *risk* while maintaining the *ambiguity*. There are neither clues as to what aspects of the character's dress or features should be included, nor examples of dialogue or particular actions. But the pupils do have a framework in which to operate in that they have to write five lines on each section and they have general headings by way of guidance. The teacher has therefore also reduced the risk that they will make a totally inappropriate response. The pupils are clear about what the teacher will expect them to produce (25 lines of writing), but it is still left to them, individually, to chose what to write (unlike the first teacher who provided words on the board). As suggested by Rosenshine *et al.* (1996), the use of cues in this way is very helpful when the object of the lesson is to develop metacognitive understanding. The second teacher is introducing the class to a set of strategies that they can use in their writing when attempting to portray characters by means of their *actions*, their *dialogue*, their *physical features* or the *narrative* itself. Furthermore, the teacher was careful not to make the scaffold too restrictive by allowing them to write five additional lines about any features of the mother that they found interesting.

The first teacher's approach in initially offering considerable guidance was presumably premised on the hope that the children would gradually grow in confidence and be able to tackle other similar character descriptions without the same degree of support. However, another important element in developing a child's self-confidence is creating the feeling that the work they have done or the ideas that they have developed are their own. Only if this is so can pupils take full credit for their achievement. The danger of the guided discovery approach is that it is often to be seen by pupils as the teacher taking over their ideas. Galton (1989) reports on one interview where children discuss this issue of ownership. One child, when asked about teachers helping them improve their ideas by offering guidance, responded:

> 'You don't feel it's your piece of work. You feel as if it is the teacher's. When you've done everything to it and you think, that is my piece of work and no one else has done anything to it, and when the teacher does something to it, it don't feel as good.' (Galton 1989: 132–3)

Thus, in summary, scaffolds where teachers take the lead, as in guided practice and modelling, do not work so well when the learning goal is to help children develop metacognitive strategies that enable them to act as independent thinkers and to self-regulate their own learning. It is the scaffolds which maintain a degree of *ambiguity* but reduce *risk* and are independent of teachers' direct intervention (such as providing cues, carrying out self-evaluation and helping pupils to review their own learning) that appear more appropriate. These scaffolds, in part, appear to be more effective because in reducing the risk they do not create a dependency on the teacher, thereby reducing the child's sense of achievement by negating his sense of ownership.

The importance of feedback

Scaffolding is a continuous process. While a teacher may structure the task initially in ways outlined in the previous paragraphs, in the course of a lesson there will be numerous occasions when pupils require help and advice. Feedback, in the widest sense, involves more than simply correcting mistakes. According to Winne and Butler, feedback is any form of 'information with which a learner can add to, overwrite, tune, or restructure information in memory, whether that information is domain knowledge, metacognitive knowledge, beliefs about self and tasks or cognitive tactics and strategies' (1994: 5740). In early behaviourist theory, feedback was seen principally as a mechanism for reinforcement in the same way as practice. However, Kulhavy (1977) has shown that it can only work in this way if the student has responded positively to the initial instruction so that the material is familiar or partially understood. Even then reinforcement may not always occur, since the pupil can chose not to accept the advice offered.

Hattie (2002) points out that feedback concerns three elements of the task, which he characterises as *feeding upwards*, *feeding back* and *feeding forward*. Feeding upwards concerns setting the learning goals. These are defined not in the narrow sense in the manner of the literacy and numeracy hours' learning objectives, but as indications to the students of what teachers expect them to know by the end of a lesson. Goals which state that by the end of a lesson pupils will be able to compare, contrast, evaluate and so on, are of this kind. When pupils have a clear understanding of the success criteria for any given task they are then able to track their performance and, providing the goals are sufficiently challenging, make appropriate changes in strategy (Locke and Latham 1990). In an English context, this accords with Black and Wiliam's conclusion that 'the provision of challenging assignments and extensive feedback leads to greater student engagement and higher achievement' (1998a: 13).

Hattie's (2002) second category, feeding back, concerns the kinds of information which allows pupils to decide how they are doing. It can either concern information about a pupil's progress or advice on what to do next. While formal assessments provide one source of this kind of feedback, it can also be given during lessons when teachers check on pupils' progress. In this situation these exchanges can develop into the third type of feedback, which *feeds forward* and is concerned with pupils' metacognitive capacities. Probing and reflecting on the use of certain strategies rather than others, identifying errors, considering the appropriateness of particular solutions, are all activities that enable pupils to acquire the knowledge required to exercise greater control over their own learning through the process of self-regulation.

Hattie (2002) also suggests that when a student is given feedback it may work at a number of different levels. The first of these concerns the pupil's self-image and usually involves praise or criticism, which is often unrelated to the quality of the performance. In Hong Kong primary classrooms, for example, when a child answers any question correctly it is often the case that the teacher and the rest of the class will give him or her the 'thumbs up sign' and chorus 'You are great, you are good'. In English classrooms praise is more muted and less frequent (Galton *et al.* 1999; Harrop and Swinson 2000). When pupils were shown a cartoon picture of a teacher helping pupils with their mathematics work and asked to write down what the teacher was saying, over two-thirds of the comments were negative, such as 'You've got it wrong', 'Do it again,' and 'You've got something right for once' (Galton 1989). Research findings show that praise, unless it is linked to specific evidence of improvement, has little effect on attainment or effort (Brophy 1981; Delin and Baumeister 1994). 'You've got three more spellings correct compared to last time – well done!' is more effective than the general, 'You've worked hard today. Give yourself a merit mark.' The latter statement tends to say more about the teacher's evaluation of the pupil's ability or effort and can have negative consequences, particularly if the pupil feels that they have made similar efforts on other occasions which have gone unnoticed. Too often praise is used as a controlling factor (Kast and Conner 1988), as when the class is told by the teacher, 'I like the way that Ian is waiting with his arms folded and ready to listen.' Not only is this likely to embarrass Ian, but it can also antagonise other members of the class towards this particular pupil. Midgley and Urdan (1992) argue that rewards such as praise should only be given in recognition of the *quality* rather than the *quantity* of a pupil's accomplishments, particularly when the task involved presents a challenge that taxes his or her abilities. Above all, the practice of seeking to encourage low achievers by praising poorer work is not recommended. This is because able students often see it as unjust and this leads them to question the teacher's credibility (Natriello and Dornbusch 1985). Furthermore, it can have a negative effect on the less-able pupil who perceives that the teacher has little confidence in the latter's capacity to do more than complete routine, easy tasks (Thompson 1997).

The second level at which feedback operates is when informing students how well they have performed on a task. Typically, this involves teachers telling pupils whether their answer is right or wrong, and for this reason it is often referred to as *correctional* feedback. In English primary classrooms teachers tend to combine corrective feedback with praise or criticism, but Bennett and Kell (1989) suggest that this reduces the attention that pupils pay to the task information. Written comments tend to have more effect than providing marks or ticks in a book (Black and Wiliam 1998a), but even then the effects seem to operate at a *surface* rather than a *deep* level that is commonly associated with the acquisition of procedural knowledge rather than understanding (Biggs and Collis 1982). For this reason it is recommended that task feedback should be combined with the third level which involves *task processing*. This includes getting pupils to spot their own mistakes (rather than pointing them out), questioning them about the appropriateness of the methods chosen, and asking for suggestions about how to approach similar tasks on subsequent occasions. According to Earley *et al.* a combination of task and task processing feedback acts as a cueing mechanism that 'appears to be a direct and powerful way of shaping an individual's task strategy' (1990: 105). On the other hand, corrective feedback alone 'may lure people into a false sense of confidence, which could have implications for long term performance.'

This leads to the final level at which feedback can operate that has to do with becoming 'metacognitively wise' through self-regulation of one's learning. Feedback about self-regulation mainly concerns the ways that pupils monitor their own task processing and is therefore closely associated with the concept of *assessment for learning* (ARG 1999; Black and Wiliam 1998b). To be effective it must go beyond getting pupils to use 'traffic lights' or 'smiley faces' to indicate the extent to which they need 'lots, little or no' help with their task. There are two important aspects of self-assessment (Paris and Winograd, 1990); the first has to do with self-appraisal and the second with self-management. The former concerns the capacity of the pupil to review their performance and the latter to regulate their behaviour in response to this performance review. Pupils may, for example, re-plan their whole approach, correct particular mistakes, or decide on a short-term 'quick-fix' solution that enables them to complete the task.

In Doyle's (1983) task-analysis framework, self-assessment involves high levels of ambiguity. The pupils' capacity to cope with challenge will determine how they deal with this uncertainty. Either they will be prepared to make the effort required by seeking hints or cues from the teacher, or they will opt for the quicker (and safer) solution by attempting to badger the teacher into providing suggestions or answers (Ryan and Pintrich 1997). According to Mueller and Dweck (1998), self-regulation feedback that emphasises effort rather than performance is much more effective. Other researchers (Covington 1992; Schunk 1983) take a different view and caution against attributing success to the pupils' hard work. This is because if some in the class have been perceived to achieve their success more easily, then those praised for their efforts may infer that the teacher thinks that their ability is somewhat limited. Brophy, in reviewing this and other research, comes to the following conclusions:

> These cautions are well taken. Ordinarily the notions that students have the ability to succeed, are making good progress, and are putting forth sufficient effort should be implied

rather than stated directly in your feedback. Effort should not be mentioned at all if it is satisfactory. If you want to express appreciation to students whose efforts are more than satisfactory do so in ways that do not imply limited ability (e.g., note their careful work, their willingness to stick with a problem until they solve it but don't tell them that they succeeded because they worked hard. With struggling students ... feedback should emphasise persistence and patience to allow time for relevant skills to develop ... Present difficult work not so much as hard, and therefore requiring strenuous effort, but as challenging them to remaining goal orientated and persist in using adaptive learning strategies. (2004: 75)

In summary, therefore, Brophy's (2004) advice is for teachers to motivate their students by telling them to save themselves from having to 'work hard' by 'working smart'. Hattie (2002) argues that the different levels of feedback (self, task, task process and self-regulation) are all involved whatever the particular goals of learning. This reflects the same approach as Moseley *et al.* where strategic and reflective thinking operates across all three of their thinking skill strands. They argue that this is because:

While the most recognisable thinking process would appear to involve a series of overlapping phases involving information gathering at the outset, a gradual building up of understanding, and ultimately productive thinking, there are likely to be many occasions when learners will come to realise that they will need to acquire more information or to revise their initial understanding. (2005: 378)

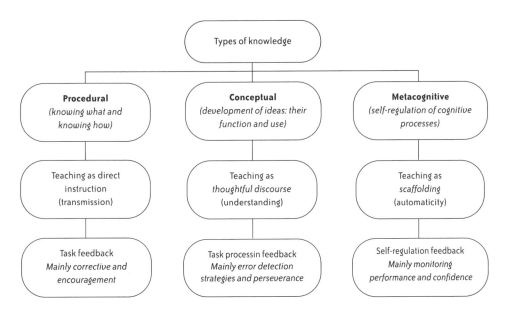

Figure **5.3** Knowledge, pedagogy and feedback

While it has already been conceded in the previous chapter that there will often be an over-lap between the acquisition of procedural knowledge, growth in understanding and the development of pupils as 'expert learners,' within any given task or topic, the preference here is to support the thesis set out by Patricia Alexander *et al.* (1991), which lays stress upon the hierarchical nature of the process. In Figure 5.3 therefore, the use of various forms of 'self-regulating' feedback are linked specifically to the 'teaching as scaffolding' strand of the framework and the kinds of high *risk*, highly *challenging* tasks which are essential for devel-oping metacognitive wisdom. Task (or surface level) feedback is most frequently used when teaching for *knowledge transmission*, task-processing feedback when the objective is primarily to teach for *understanding*, while self-regulating feedback is most appropriate when used alongside non-directed scaffolding to help children learn how to control their own thinking. However, every level of feedback has implications for pupils' motivation because the attribu-tions that pupils take away as a result of receiving feedback can affect their self-image in either positive or negative ways. This is because, as Gipps (1994) argues, feedback is both *descriptive* in that it provides information about the different levels (task, task processing, self-regulation) and is in every case *evaluative* (concerned with self). At task level this evalua-tive component is mainly designed to offer encouragement, while at the task processing stage the main object is to encourage pupils, in Brophy's (2004: 75) words, to '*work smarter*'. At the self-regulation stage it is more important that the evaluative component helps pupils to maintain their confidence, particularly when the self-monitoring process suggests that the chosen strategy may not be working (McCallum *et al.* 2002; Tunstall and Gipps 1996).

Hattie (2002) also summarises the results of a large number of meta-analyses on the effects of various forms of feedback on attainment. This form of research review combines the results of a number of studies having similar characteristics, and attempts to produce an overall estimate of their effectiveness by means of an *effect size*. This measure is preferred to stating statistical significance levels, since the latter are heavily influenced by sample size and may represent little in the way of educational value. Effect size takes account of the average spread of scores in assessing gains in achievement, and it has been suggested that a value of 0.5 represents the equivalent of a year's progress (or in National Curriculum terms, one-third of a level). Hattie's (2002) analysis is shown in Table 5.1.

Table **5.1** Effect sizes associated with various types of feedback
Source: Compiled from data in Hattie (2002)

Variable	No. of Studies	Effect size
All forms of feedback	4157	0.95
Cues, prompts, etc.	89	1.10
Reinforcement	19	0.94
Corrective	1149	0.37
Delayed v. immediate	178	0.34
Reward	223	0.31
Immediate v. delayed	398	0.24
Sanctions	89	0.20
Praise	388	0.14

Overall, in studies where it was not possible to establish the exact form of feedback, but in classes where levels were high, the effect size was in the order of two-thirds of a National Curriculum Level. In more specific instances, and in order of effectiveness, providing feedback in the form of cues (hints, questions about the use of a particular strategy) as part of task processing and self-regulation has maximum impact (effect size = 1.10). This is followed by feedback which acts as reinforcement (that is, spurs on the pupils to greater effort rather than being seen as a comment on their ability), which has a value of 0.94. These two components far outweigh the contribution of corrective feedback (0.37), rewards (stars, merit stickers, house points, and so on) with an effect size of 0.31, and either punishment (0.20) or praise (0.14). A further issue to emerge from this analysis is the timing of feedback (delayed or immediate). Kurlik and Kurlick (1988) found that if the feedback was largely to do with 'teaching for transmission', then immediate feedback is marginally more beneficial (immediate v. delayed = 0.28), while, with testing, delayed feedback is to be preferred (0.36). Much depends on whether further opportunities to make use of the feedback are available, and this accords with Nuthall and Alton-Lee's (1995) conclusions, reported in Chapter 3. There it was reported that students required several exposures to material over the course of two or three days in order to ensure that a high degree of information was retained over time. A more important determinant would appear to be the complexity of the task. When the task is difficult (in terms of challenge and risk) it is more effective to delay feedback. Hattie (2002) reports on a study by Clariana *et al.* (2000) who coded tasks as either easy, mid-range or difficult. The effect size for delayed feedback with easy items was −0.06, for medium range ones 0.35, but for the most difficult it reached 1.17. One possible explanation lies in the exchange reported in the previous chapter, where pupils said that when working collaboratively they preferred the teacher to delay giving help until group members had formed some opinions they could defend collectively. Too early an intervention was regarded as a 'teacher take-over' and made pupils feel that they no longer 'owned their ideas'.

Some concluding comments

Throughout this and the previous two chapters it has been repeatedly stressed that the various teaching approaches, based as they are on different models of learning, are interlinked. There will be times, for example during a lesson involving collaborative group work, where some direct instruction may be necessary. In planning lessons it is therefore important to balance these different approaches according to the knowledge demands which frame the learning goals of a particular lesson or topic. This is particularly true of lessons where the tasks are of a higher intellectual order and the aim is also to encourage children to think for themselves. The teacher first needs to consider what procedures are necessary in order to accomplish this goal. The children may not already have mastered certain procedures (or they may need reinforcing), and if this is the case these should be taught directly. When the cognitive requirement of the task involves an element of peer regulation or self-regulation, then it is usually necessary to provide a greater degree of scaffolding if pupils are to accomplish the task successfully. Key concepts also need to be identified and the extent to which

Learning goals

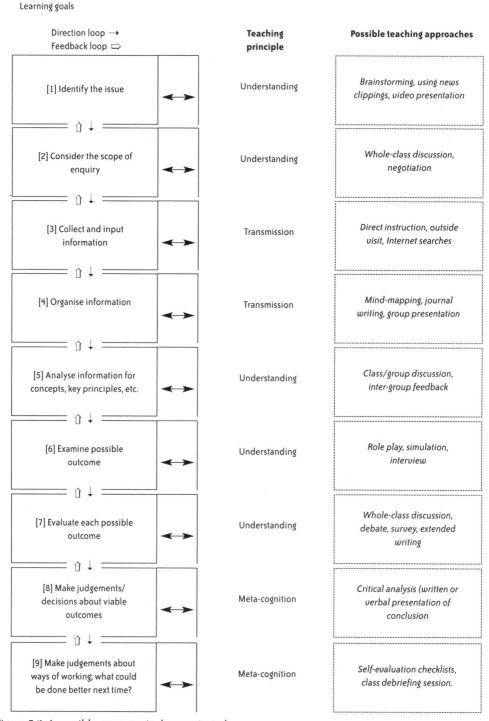

Figure **5.4** A possible cross-curriculum project plan
Source: Adapted from Chapter 4, *Senior Secondary Curriculum Guide*, Hong Kong Curriculum Development Institute.

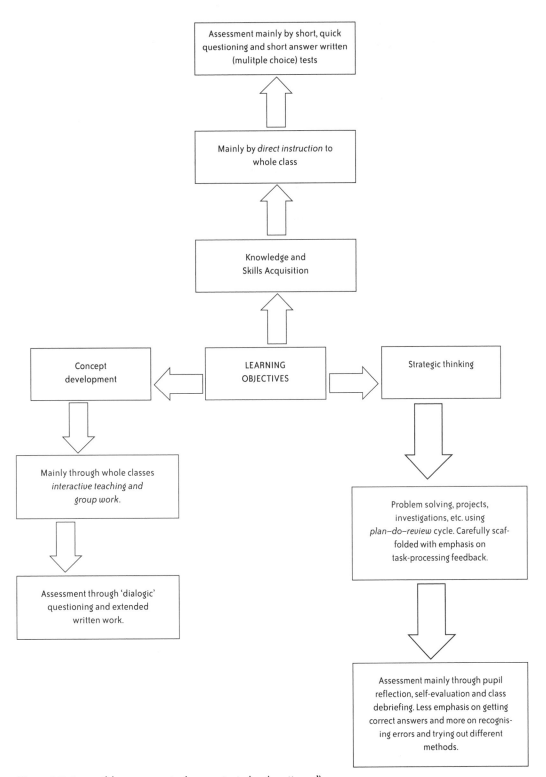

Figure **5.4** A possible cross-curriculum project plan (*continued*)

the children's thinking will need to be stimulated through challenging questioning, antici-pated in the light of the teacher's previous knowledge of the class. The dilemma, whether to intervene or simply to mediate the children's growing understanding of a particular con-cept, will not be amenable to hard and fast rules but will be largely determined by the result of previous experience. Here again, however, teachers need to be very careful in making these judgements in that they see the children 'as they are' and not in accordance with existing stereotypes or a particular set of personal beliefs.

Figure 5.4 illustrates a possible way of setting out a topic plan with these principles in mind. In the left hand column are the learning goals and in the right hand column the possi-ble teaching approaches that could be used to accomplish these. This framework can be checked against the principles outlined at the end of the previous chapter in order to see if it conforms to the proposed learning–teaching model. For example, it can be seen that under the first column both the first and second learning goals obey the initial maxim required for teaching for understanding, that *investigation should generally precede instruction*. Looking down the list of teaching approaches we can check that the following axioms concerning the *prepon-derance of talk* with the *majority of it taking place between pupils* is also fulfilled. Taking into account the eighth and ninth of the learning goals, it can be seen that these concern teaching for metacognition where the teacher should check that the planned tasks are scaffolded in ways which *do not require too much teacher guidance*, thus avoiding pupil dependency.

Finally there is a question of assessment. If the learning objectives are primarily con-cerned with knowledge and skills acquisition, then the teaching will occur mainly through direct instruction to the whole class and assessment will consist mainly of rapid, quick questioning and short, written answers such as multiple choice tests. However, if the learn-ing goals are concerned with developing concepts, this will take place mainly through whole-class dialogic teaching and/or collaborative group work. The assessment will either be conducted verbally by means of detailed questioning or through extended written work, since it will be necessary to probe the extent to which the concepts are embedded and have led to increased understanding. This is done by checking that students can apply these ideas to novel situations. However, when the aim is to develop metacognitive skills so that pupils can think strategically, then the teaching is likely to emphasise careful, non-directed scaf-folding with an emphasis on task processing and self-regulating feedback. Here assessment must occur mainly through pupil reflection and self-evaluation, since there is less interest in whether pupils produce correct answers and more emphasis on the thinking processes used (whether the pupils were able to recognise their errors and to arrive at reasonable decisions about the most appropriate methods to apply). This approach is consistent with the princi-ples that govern Assessment for Learning (Black and Wiliam 1998d: Black *et al.* 2003). AfL seeks to involve pupils in peer assessment so that they can explain how they arrived at an answer and discuss how they can improve their performance on a future occasion. In this situation, questions such as 'Where have you got to?', 'What do you think may have gone wrong?', 'What are you doing to do next?' have less to do with reinforcement and correction and are more about self-regulation. As Watkins (2005) argues so cogently, for these strate-gies to be effective the culture of primary classrooms needs to change so that they cease to be dominated by the current pressure to perform and become places where both students and teacher feel themselves to be part of a learning community: one where performance does not necessarily equal learning. In such classrooms teachers can explore with their pupils the emotional conditions of learning as well as the cognitive aspects. In such a climate it becomes possible to hold discussions about 'fear of failure' by asking the children what it feels like when I (the teacher) choose you (the pupil) to answer a question in front of the rest of the class. Spot-checks during lessons, such as those devised by MacBeath and McGlynn (2002) where children indicate whether they are happy, bored, concentrating, anxious, etc, are also an important element in this environment. Teachers are fond of telling children that they learn by mistakes. The children appear not to believe this message when faced with the emphasis on levels, ticks in books, and the predominance of corrective feedback in most lessons. Teaching pupils to be metacognitively wise is therefore extremely difficult in a culture that emphasises performance, since failure is inevitably attributed to lack of ability in this situation. This issue of the classroom environment will be discussed in the concluding chapter along with a number of other questions that teachers have raised about the implementation of the strategies outlined in this and the previous chapter. Before that, however, some of the issues surrounding the use of group work will be explored.

Key references

Alexander, P. Schallert, D. and Hare, V. (1991) Coming to terms: how researchers in learning and literacy talk about knowledge, *Review of Educational Research*, 61(3): 315–43.

Doyle, W. (1983) Academic work, *Review of Educational Research*, 53: 159–99.

Moseley, D., Elliott, J., Gregson, M. and Higgins, S. (2005) Thinking skill frameworks for use in education and training, *British Educational Research Journal*, 31(3): 367–90.

Rosenshine, B., Meister, C. and Chapman, S. (1996) Teaching students to generate questions: a review of intervention studies, *Review of Educational Research*, 66(2) 181–221.

Chapter 6

Group Work in the Primary Classroom

In terms of strict continuity, this discussion of grouping and group work should have followed immediately after Chapter 4, which dealt with teaching for understanding. The central theme of that chapter, the creation of a classroom which encourages *thoughtful discourse*, applies not only to whole-class discussions but also to the times when pupils are required to converse among themselves in small groups. However, there is also value in placing the chapter immediately after the one where the issues concerning metacognitive learning were explored. This is because group work, if it is to be effective, requires pupils to gain an understanding of what it is to become a *group person* in the same way that they need to understand what it is to be a scientist, writer, historian and so forth. Furthermore, to be a good 'group person' pupils also have to possess certain procedural skills and these, in accordance with the proposed model, are best acquired through the process of direct instruction. There are also important concepts that need to be developed, such as those embedded in the idea of *cooperative learning*. Teaching children to work effectively together in small groups therefore incorporates most of the principles outlined in the previous chapters, and thus provides a useful illustration of how an approach based on these principles can work in practice.

Is working in groups an effective pedagogy?

There is certainly a strong body of research that supports the view that working in groups can improve both students' academic performance and attitudes, although most of these empirical studies have been undertaken outside of the United Kingdom. A number of reviews and meta-analyses (Cohen, 1994; Johnson *et al.* 1983; Sharan, 1980; Slavin, 1983; Webb, 1985) have established not only large to moderate effect sizes in terms of attainment when cooperative structures for learning are compared to competitive and individualistic ones, but have also indicated other important gains relating to social cohesion, motivation and improvements in self esteem. Recent studies in the United Kingdom, as part of the Teaching and Learning Research Programme (TLRP) initiative, have shown substantial gains at Key Stage 2 (science) and Key Stage 3 (English and mathematics), particularly when the tests attempt to measure understanding rather than procedural knowledge (Blatchford *et al.*

2005). Light and Littleton (1994) and Mercer *et al.* (2004) also concur that working in groups appears to have the greatest impact on pupil performance when the goal is to develop reasoning and problem-solving skills. Despite such evidence, the use of cooperative groups in English primary schools continues to be what in the 1970s, Galton (1980) described as a 'neglected art'. Twenty years after the original ORACLE study, a replication found that children in Key Stage 2 classes were still mainly seated in groups but working on individual or whole-class tasks (Galton *et al.* 1999). More recent research by Baines *et al.* (2003) supports this finding.

In primary school classrooms, seating children in groups around small tables came to the fore in the late 1960s and early 1970s. This coincided with the abolition of the 11+ examination for selection to grammar schools as a result of the move to comprehensive schooling. The change was mostly a pragmatic means of coping with the consequent shift away from streaming in the junior school (Barker Lunn 1984) that appeared to require pupils of similar ability to be grouped together for certain subjects, particularly mathematics and reading. This trend appears to have been maintained, despite the pressure on primary schools in recent years to setting by ability and within and across classes. According to Harlen and Malcolm (1999), about one-quarter of mathematics and one-seventh of English classes were set at Key Stage 2 but in most other subjects pupils operated in mixed ability, mixed gender groups. More recently, Kutnick *et al.* (2002) 'mapped' the use of within-class groups in 187 Year 2 and Year 4 classrooms. Around 49 per cent of the pupils' experience consisted of working in small groups, followed by whole-class (21 per cent) larger groups of between 7 and 10 members (11 per cent) and dyads (10 per cent). Groups were now more likely to be based on ability, which has distorted the previous common practice of having equal numbers of boys and girls in each team (presumably for assisting their social and emotional development). Low-attaining boys and high-attaining girls were now often grouped together. These findings are similar to those of Pollard *et al.* (2000).

However, whatever the grouping arrangement, a consistent finding linking the research in primary classes across several decades is that while pupils may *sit in groups* they rarely *work as groups*. For the most part when sitting in groups pupils either work as a class or individually on practice and revision tasks. This arrangement has not always been a productive one, since when pupils did talk to one another in their groups the conversations tend to involve 'social' rather than task-related matters (Hastings and Schweiso 1995). For this reason it is increasingly being recommended that other seating arrangements may be more suitable for tasks involving whole-class discussion or for individual seat work (Hastings and Chantry 2002).

Among the factors which may cause practitioners to desist from encouraging pupils to work together in their groups is the perception by some teachers of a loss of control over the learning environment. It is often difficult to be certain that talk among pupils in groups is productive, or even on task, and this compares unfavourably with the situation that usually pertains during whole-class discussions where pupils speak only when requested to do so by the teacher (Galton and Williamson 1992). It is also sometimes difficult to decide on the appropriateness of the task and the degree of structure required, whether, for example, there is need for interdependence so that no group can complete a task without a contribution from all members, or whether more open-ended, discovery-based activities can produce more higher-order exchanges (Bennett and Dunne 1992; Cohen, 1994).

Size and composition of groups can also create difficulties. Teachers tend to see the need to mix abilities or to include pupils with behaviour problems as a further obstacle to cooperative learning rather than seeing the use of groups as a means of solving such difficulties (Cowie *et al.* 1994). While, in the main, the research provides evidence of gains for all groups of students (Johnson and Johnson 1985; Slavin 1995; Palincsar and Herrenkohl 1999), some studies such as Sheppard (1993) report that gifted pupils were less attracted to working cooperatively in mixed-ability groups. Views about the benefits for disruptive pupils are also mixed. Putnam *et al.* (1996) reported positive socialising effects for such children as a result of cooperative group activities, while others such as Brinton *et al.* (1998) claim that aggression or withdrawal is a more typical response. Social interdependence through cooperative learning is also said to produce greater intrinsic and achievement motivation (Johnson and Johnson 1987), but these findings don't take into account the effects of certain personality factors. Webb (1989), for example, found that extraverts were more likely to interact in groups, while findings by Entwistle (1977) suggest that anxious pupils learn best from highly structured materials, so that the more open-ended problem-solving approaches developed by Sharan and Sharan (1992) may be less appropriate. This last reservation, however, may apply to a greater degree in the case of secondary pupils.

A further difficulty confronting the class teacher concerns the organisation of group work within everyday classroom settings. Most of the studies cited in the literature obtained positive results under conditions where a degree of control operated. Under these experimental arrangements the class all worked in their groups on the same or similar tasks at the same point in time. Furthermore, during the initial trial phase the teacher could often count on help from a number of 'ready-made' assistants in the form of members from the research team. These conditions are somewhat different from those faced in a typical primary classroom. There, a teacher may at any one time have to manage several different activities and respond to various requests for help while simultaneously dealing with a behaviour or some other routine management issue. Although other studies have focused on providing specific help in certain aspects of group work, such as decision making (Howe and Tolmie 2003) and improving the quality of talk (Mercer 2000), there are few accounts of researchers attempting to work alongside teachers to support the use of group work under these typical conditions: an exception being Rudduck *et al.* (1996), although the pupils studied were mostly from the lower secondary school. The idea behind developing a *social pedagogy* of group work (Kutnick *et al.* 2002) is to help teachers develop ways of implementing group working successfully within these everyday typical classroom settings.

Some key ideas about group work

There are several possible reasons why group work produces improvements in pupils' attainment and attitude. Cohen and Lotan (1995) argue that working in groups can provide pupils with opportunities to appreciate the qualities of some team members who may not stand out during whole-class discussions. This helps to explain the findings from various reviews in which the self-esteem of 'low status' pupils (particularly in terms of ability, social class and race) improved as a result of group work. This explanation is often coupled with the use of the 'team-games tournament' approach developed by Robert Slavin (1995). In this form of group work each group plays against each other for a reward. However, since the group's score is the sum of all its team's individual contributions, it is necessary for the more knowledgeable to coach the weaker members. In this manner group work promotes both *positive interdependence* (we work as a team; we sink or swim together; we haven't succeeded until we can all do it and so on) and *individual accountability* (the team builds and shares its skills so that what the team can do one day each member will be able to do on their own the next). Others (Johnson and Johnson 1987) dispute the need for competitive structures, arguing that it is the sense of cooperating together (being valued as good group member) that provides the drive to succeed.

From a cognitive perspective, however, it is the *social constructivist* ideas of Vygotsky, which were discussed in Chapter 3, that hold the key to the group's success. In the same way that a more knowledgeable adult can help a pupil to move through the *zone of proximal (or potential) development*, so too can a more knowledgeable peer, providing the conversations within the group can move beyond mere descriptive talk to that of explanation and genuine debate (Webb 1989). However, there are relational issues to contend with if the cognitive conflict induced by such debate is to be accompanied by the twin processes of *construction and re-construction* that are a necessary prerequisite for developing improved understanding. If, for example, the group has some members who have little respect for views of others, then the power relationships that stem from this inequality may mean that the weaker members become submissive partners. As a result, no new joint perspective is likely to emerge from such discussions and only *surface* learning will take place. For Kutnick and Manson (1998), therefore, the *relational* aspects of working in groups are crucial. Without the development of mutually supportive social relationships between group members, so that they learn to trust and respect each other's viewpoints, little *deep* learning will occur (Hall 1994). Such relationships can be developed through the appropriate use of techniques such as *circle time* (Bliss *et al.* 1995), but can also be built into the group activities as part of a training programme.

Training children to work in groups

One significant factor in successful business organisations is teamwork (Handy 1993), and it is not surprising to find that considerable effort and time is spent in training new recruits to become effective team members (Bee and Bee 1997). It comes as something of a surprise, therefore, to find that even when teachers are 'group work enthusiasts' it is often the case that no training in group work skills is given (Galton and Williamson 1992). Indeed, Kutnick *et al.*'s (2005) review of the literature could only find one evaluation of a training programme at primary level (Kagan 1988), although various manuals are readily available (Cowie and Rudduck 1991; Kingsley-Mills *et al.* 1992). Part of the reason appears to be a belief, fashioned out of a misinterpretation of the notion of Piagetian *readiness*, that the acquisition of these core skills comes about mainly through the pupils' interaction with suitable tasks rather than through direct instruction (Galton and Williamson 1992).

Table **6.1** Key phases of group work training

Phase	Skills and dispositions	Main approach
Beginning	Developing trust and confidence Learning the group rules	Circle time, role play, class debriefing
Middle	Communicating effectively Active listening Maintainance role Decision making Handling conflict	Coaching and practice Group/class discussion
End	Becoming a better group person	Self-evaluation checklists

Most training manuals break down the training into five key phases, as set out in Table 6.1.

The setting of rules is important in that as far as possible pupils should 'own' the rules by having the opportunity to decide for themselves, as in the following exercise.

Group rules

The aim of the exercise is for the children to arrive at a set of rules for conducting discussion in their group. It is important that pupils feel the rules are not imposed by the teacher. Here is an example:

Children sit in groups of 4/6. They are asked to discuss the six most important rules for making the group work well (10 minutes). Each group reports back and the teacher writes down their suggestions, ticking any statement which is repeated. The final six rules should be written on a poster and put up on the wall. If too difficult a task for some children, the teacher picks a list of rules and ask groups to decide if each one is fair (for example, 'If you want to be heard, shout' or 'Only agree with your friends' or 'Everyone should get a turn to speak' and so on).

It is important to reinforce the rules within different contexts so that transfer of learning takes place. Too often this exercise is done during PSHE lessons, but the rules need to be adjusted when, say, children are doing a scientific experiment where each member of the group may have different responsibilities (each taking turns in conducting the experiment under different conditions to gather sufficient data for a bar chart). Such an activity is very different from one in English where pupils may be writing a short play to perform in front of the rest of the class. Dawes *et al.* (2000) give the following examples as likely outcomes of the above exercise in drawing up a list of rules:

- We share ideas.
- We take turns to speak.
- We try to agree.
- We respect other people's ideas.

- We listen to each other.

- We involve everybody.

- We don't shout or get angry.

- We talk one at a time.

In the matter of developing trust and confidence, the following activities are suggested by Kingsley Mills *et al.* (1992).

Establishing trust

The following are examples of helpful exercises. Class debriefing is essential.

- Each group is given a bag and told there may be a nasty creature inside. Pupils are asked to tell each other how they would feel if they had to place their hand inside the bag.

- Each person in the group picks another member who is not a special friend and completes the sentence 'Today I have noticed …'. The group discusses what new things they have found out about each other.

- Prepare an outline drawing (of a tree, house, etc). A group of 4 is given colouring pencils (red, green, yellow, blue) all tied together by means of short pieces of string. Pupils have to complete the picture using all the colours.

Developing communication skills

Once this initial training has been completed, the next stage involves improving the quality of the interaction within the groups. The three important elements are those of *communicating clearly* as a speaker, *helping* another group member to improve communication through the use of prompts and *active listening*. Again several examples of activities designed to improve the pupils' capacity to engage in 'thoughtful discourse' are offered.

Effective speaking I

Pupils need to learn how to communicate information and ideas to others so that they can be clearly understood. It is important initially for pupils to appreciate that talking 'at' is less effective than talking 'with' other group members. The following exercise can be used as a basis for class discussion.

Ask a pupil to come out to the front of the class and instruct the class to draw a figure made up of squares. The pupil has his/her back to the class and no questions are allowed. Pupils compare the results while the teacher displays the figure on the OHP. The exercise is repeated with another pupil and another drawing, but this time the pupil faces the class, who are allowed to ask questions. The class discusses the advantages and disadvantages of the two methods of communicating.

Depending on the age of the pupils more complex diagrams (using circles, rectangles, triangles) can be constructed.

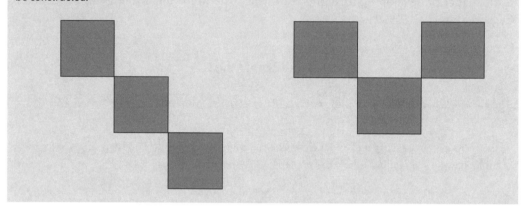

Out of this exercise should come a series of rules for effective speaking, which can be added to the rules for being a 'good group person'. Practice and class debriefing is essential if the procedures are to become firmly embedded in the conversation. With younger pupils, as in the Hong Kong P1 classes (aged 6 years) observed by the author, children are taught simply to add the word 'because' whenever they make a suggestion or offer a solution, while other members of the group are taught to say 'That's interesting. Please say more', by way of response.

Effective speaking II

Good speaking behaviour in groups.

● Stops every so often to check if audience is following (for example 'Is that OK?').

● Gives reasons or explanations for instructions/ideas (for example, 'I decided to stop running because …').

● Considers views of others in the group (for example, 'Thank you for that. Let's add that to the list of things to do.').

● Offers examples to make a point clear (for example, 'You have to get as near as possible without the person seeing you, like a tiger which is trying to creep up on its prey.').

● Makes certain that everyone has a chance to put their point of view (for example, 'Who else wants to say something?').

Some of the above aspects of speaking are quite complex and the teacher needs to judge what is and what is not appropriate for a particular class or age group.

Helpful questions to speakers

Others in the group need to help the speaker present his/her ideas by asking relevant questions. This is best practised as a class with the teacher questioning a pupil and then getting pupils to ask the teacher questions. Questions should:

- Clarify: 'What do you mean?', 'Please explain?', 'Can you say more about that please?'

- Seek evidence: 'How do you/we know that?'

- Look at implications: 'Where does that get us?', 'What can we work out from what you've just said?'

- Explore alternatives: 'Do we all think the same?', 'Do we all agree?' (If some disagree then 'What do you think?' and so on.)

Again teachers need to decide just what is possible for particular classes and age groups. The third component in developing the skills of conducting thoughtful discourse involves becoming an active listener. The class can explore this aspect of communication through the following role play. Although initially the pupils exaggerate the nodding, smiling and staring into each other's faces, the movements do become more controlled and natural as two-way conversations develop.

BECOMING AN ACTIVE LISTENER

Pupils need to do more than listen passively. They must learn how to encourage others in the group who may be shy, and also how to help others to explain their ideas more fully. This starter exercise seems to work well.

Ask a pupil to come out and tell you, the teacher, about a recent event (for example, what he or she had for dinner, what he or she did at the weekend). The teacher sits on a chair and displays all the usual signs of inattention (fidgets, looks away from the speaker, yawns and so on). The teacher then asks class if they thought he or she was a good listener. If not, why not?

The exercise is repeated with another pupil, but this time teacher listens carefully (eye contact, nods appreciatively and so on). The class in pairs take turns to practise being 'good' listeners.

Again a series of appropriate rules should emerge from this and similar role play in which the following are likely to be included:

- Maintaining eye contact, smiling or shaking the head at the right time.

- Making encouraging comments: 'Oh yes!', 'That's interesting.', 'Do go on.'

- Asking for clarification: 'I'm not sure that I understand. Please tell me more.'

- Not rushing to fill silences.

- Not finishing off speaker's sentences in anticipation of what he or she is trying to say.

- Not interrupting or over-shouting the speaker.

Maintenance strategies and taking decisions

Groups often go wrong because pupils move off the point or lose track of time, and teachers find this situation difficult to cope with because they are often uncertain as to the reason. This sometimes leads to resentment on the part of pupils, as when the teacher, on discovering that the group has not finished the task, accuses them of time wasting. Pupils therefore need help in identifying key maintenance tasks. This can include:

- *Practical*: fetching equipment, making measurements and so on.

- *Timekeeping*: making sure tasks get finished, not too much time is wasted and so on. ('How much time have we left?', 'What else have we still to do?')

- *Summarising*: ('Where have we got to?')

- *Organising*: Allocating different tasks, making sure everybody gets a say, has a turn.

It is important to make sure that different pupils get to practise different roles so that, for example, one pupil isn't always the organising leader. Again in Hong Kong classrooms teachers tend to organise classes of younger pupils into groups by colour (red group, blue group and so on) and fruit (apple group, banana group and so on) for different activities (colour = differentiated ability; fruit = mixed ability) and by number (for membership). It is then a fairly easy task to have the number one group member as this week's organiser, number two as timekeeper and so forth.

One of the most difficult training activities concerns decision making. Most pupils, when asked how they should take decisions will reply 'By voting'. While voting can sometimes be justified, as a last resort, it is far preferable for interpersonal relationships if 'nobody wins everything and nobody loses all' (Gordon 1974). Pupils who lose the vote may become unhappy and either take no further interest or, worse, become obstructive. Pupils should therefore be encouraged to seek solutions by:

- *Comparing*: 'Where do we agree/disagree?'

- *Prioritising*: 'Which is the most important thing?'

- *Compromising*: 'What if we said . . . ?'

● *Placing limits*: 'Most of us thought this, but others pointed out that . . .'

Handling disagreements

At primary stage, dealing with potential conflict is best done within the framework of class debriefings rather than by role play, which may be more appropriate for secondary school students (Kingsley-Mills *et al.* 1992). Pupils need to be helped to understand the effects of

CONFLICT STYLES	
Name........................ Place a tick against the style (or styles, not more than 3) you think most applies to this person/yourself.	
Avoiding (tortoise)	You avoid conflict at all costs. You believe it is pointless to try to resolve conflicts. It is better to withdraw, to retreat into your shell and nurse your feelings.
Smoothing (cuddly toy)	You try always to calm things down and restore relationships. You try to look for things in common rather than deal with the issue causing conflict.
Forcing (shark)	You try to get your own way at all costs. Winning is most important. Losing equals weakness. You don't care if others dislike you as a result.
Compromising (fox)	You bargain so you can find middle ground. Your assumption is that splitting the difference is the only reasonable solution.
Problem solving (owl)	You value shared goals and relationships. You seek a solution cooperatively so that from conflict can come improved relationships.

Figure **6.1** Example worksheet for dealing with behaviour problems

aggressive behaviour on others and to learn the basic elements of assertiveness (being able to say what one wants by being *specific*, *direct*, stating one's *feelings* while staying *calm* and avoiding sarcasm and so on). A useful starting point is for the Teacher to use the worksheet shown in Figure 6.1 (simplified if necessary) as the basis for discussion.

It should be clear from the above discussion that training pupils for working in groups requires a long-term strategy in which the emphasis in the training shifts over the course of the pupil's time in primary school. This requires a *pedagogic development* plan as part of a whole-school strategy. Key Stage 1, for example, might concentrate on rules of group work and some of the simpler communication skills, while at Key Stage 2 pupils should be able to devise their own maintenance strategies with little help from the teacher and begin to understand the reasons why 'blocking' or aggressive behaviour sometimes occurs. The following exchange, admittedly recorded in a Year 7 class as part of the TLRP group work *Spring* (Social Pedagogical Research into Grouping) Project (Blatchford *et al.* 2005), illustrates how, with training, pupils can become much more sensitive to each other's problems. The interview begins by speaking to Daniel, who tends not to get too involved:

Interviewer: When the teacher says, 'Right I want you to get into your groups' what do you think?

Daniel: Boring lesson. Supposed to have to think.

Interviewer: Would it be more boring if you did it as a class?

Daniel: Yeah. But it wouldn't matter because I'd just sit there and do nothing still.

Interviewer: So you can't opt out?

Daniel: I don't get myself involved. I never do.

Other pupils in the same group, however, seem to have worked out Daniel's problem, as instanced by the following exchange:

Michael: If we're in a group and had somebody who didn't think they were as clever and had an idea and the person who they thought was cleverest also had an idea they'd immediately go with the person who had the cleverest idea.

Gareth: That's what Daniel's like.

Michael: Because Daniel thinks he isn't any good at English but he is quite good.

Interviewer: Do you tell him that?

Michael: Yeah. We do tell him and he comes up with some good ideas sometimes. But if I say something that's different to him then he'll immediately just go all wobbly.

Gareth: He doesn't believe it.

It is clear from the latter exchange that both Michael and Gareth are beginning to gain metacognitive wisdom about what it means to be a good group person.

Becoming an expert group person

Developing an understanding of what is required to work effectively in a group and of being sensitive to the needs and problems of other team members requires more than direct instruction in how to be a good listener, communicator, maintenance person and so forth. Pupils have to be able to develop their own strategies for dealing with problems as they arise, to be able to assess their effectiveness and to seek out further improvements. This is the stuff of metacognitive thinking and, as discussed in the previous chapter, needs careful scaffolding. The two main approaches involve regular debriefings by the teacher and independent self-evaluations by the group members.

Earlier in the book it was argued that, as teachers, we are good at telling pupils *what* to do but that we don't often explain *why* they are being asked to do a particular task, nor do we give pupils opportunities to reflect on the finished activity. Part of developing pupils' metacognitive awareness of working in groups involves briefing, that is, explaining why the task is being done in groups (for example, more efficient way of collecting information, more chance of coming up with a solution by sharing ideas and so on). It also affords a good opportunity to remind the class of the group rules and to stress particular aspects of group working (for example, listening, turn-taking, etc). This is followed by a debriefing session where the groups can be asked questions along the lines of: 'Did the task work well?',

---

WORKING IN A GROUP

Did I like working in this group?

☺   😐   ☹

Did others listen to me?

☺   😐   ☹

Did I listen to others?

☺   😐   ☹

Did everyone get a turn at speaking?

☺   😐   ☹

How can I be a better group person next time?

....

....

'Did the groups work well?', 'What would you change next time?'

Self-evaluation sheets need to be used sparingly, otherwise pupils may become bored with the task of filling them in and give their responses scant consideration. The two examples that follow show how the questions can become more sophisticated as the training develops over time. In the first case, Key Stage 1 pupils could be asked to evaluate their listening skills by selecting symbols.

By the time that pupils have reached Year 6, however, the questions can be more probing and can collect information about the use of maintenance strategies, decision making and ways of dealing with potential conflict. Among possible evaluation questions are:

- How well did we work together as a group?
- How good were we at making decisions?
- How well did we organise the different tasks?
- How well did we respond to the group leader's instructions?
- How well did we time-keep?
- How well did we paraphrase and summarise?
- Who did I help? Why?
- Who did I block? Why?
- What am I going to do about it next time?

As pupils gain confidence and trust in each other, the evaluation can form part of a group exercise. Pupils fill in the evaluation sheets individually and then share their judgements with other group members in an effort to arrive at a consensus about their overall performance. It is through these kinds of activity that pupils begin to understand what is required of them when working together in groups.

Some frequently asked questions and problems

Discussions among teachers about the use of group work quickly identify a number of questions, problems and key concerns. The following are the most common.

Size and composition

Anything up to six in the group seems to work well (Dunne and Bennett 1990), but others suggest keeping the numbers down to four at the start when younger children are beginning to develop their relational skills (Daniels 1994). Even numbers (2, 4 or 6) are often useful because they allow pairs to share different activities, as in jigsaw grouping (Aronson and Patnoe 1997). Large friendship groups can lead to social rather than task talk (MacDonald et al. 2002), although this study was solely concerned with musical collaboration. The opposite view is taken by Rudduck in Galton et al. (2003); she has evidence that with the help of briefing and de-briefing, pupils can become quite sophisticated in the matter of choosing working partners and can distinguish between friends 'who you can play with' and those 'who get you into trouble' when you work together. A mix of able and less able, confident and less confident pupils appears to be more important. A useful strategy is to allow pairs of friends to work together and then join them with another pair of different ability/gender, although Kutnick and Kington (2005) suggest that boy–boy friendship pairings tend to be less successful that girl friendship pairs.

Reluctant participants

Some pupils don't like sharing. Teachers may feel it preferable to ignore such behaviour at first rather than draw attention to it. Eventually non-cooperation can have a negative effect on the other group members who may feel that they are not being listened to. Faced with this situation, teachers should choose practical tasks which allow individual contributions, which then have to be linked together for a common presentation, rather than those where everyone is involved in working towards a common goal. Shy pupils can usually be dealt with by beginning activities in friendship pairs, but pupils who are *work shy* and leave it to others in the group to do the work are more problematic. The use of Slavin's (1995) team-games approach can sometimes be useful, in that each individual contribution has to count towards the group's total score. Otherwise, the issue needs to be explored and resolved through the use of debriefing and self-evaluation activities.

Choice of task

As stated earlier in the chapter, two of the main aims of using group work are to develop what Johnson and Johnson (2000) term *positive interdependence* and *individual accountability*. Certain tasks tend to emphasise one of these dimensions more than the other. For this reason Galton and Williamson (1992) and Bennett and Dunne (1992) have tended to distinguish between *cooperative* and *collaborative* tasks, although the terms tend to be used interchangeably elsewhere in the literature. The difference can be defined as follows:

- *Collaborative groups*: emphasise social interdependence, where pupils work cooperatively to complete a common task (for example, pupils have to act out a chapter in a story, deciding who does what and which bits to select; discuss the pros and cons of having chips taken off the school dinner menu; have to design an apparatus to time 2 minutes using empty plastic bottles, sand and other scrap material).

- *Cooperative groups*: emphasise individual accountability, where pupils work independently on their own tasks as a contribution to a common goal (for example, each pupil makes their own drawing for a collage; pupils investigate different sources of information – books, brochures websites and so on – in preparing a holiday package for a party of pensioners; pupils investigate the effect of temperature on dissolving a solid into water, with each person covering a particular temperature range).

There are also seating groups where pupils work on their own individual topic but help each other informally by checking answers, making suggestions and so forth. While research tends to show that such groups tend to promote off-task behaviour (Hastings and Schweiso 1995), it can be argued that once pupils have been trained to work together (and helping each other in the above ways has been legitimised in the classroom rules) then engaged time increases. This is certainly the experience of the *Spring* Project researchers (Blatchford *et al.* 2005). Tasks can also be 'open' or 'closed', giving rise to different levels of ambiguity and risk (Doyle 1983). A common misconception is that group tasks should always be open ones. Galton and Williamson (1992), however, found that such tasks were not very effective in the early stages when groups were still building confidence in working together and learning to trust each other. In these circumstances group members tended to opt for the first solution offered as a means of avoiding having to produce alternative suggestions of their own. In the earlier interview extract, Michael illustrates the situation perfectly when he remarks that someone like Daniel 'who doesn't think he's any good at English' would 'immediately go' with the cleverest person's idea. Galton and Williamson (1992) found that a closed task (with a degree of ambiguity), which forces the group to go back and check the appropriateness of the answer against a set of criteria provided by the teacher, is generally more effective. Over a period of time, however, teachers should increase the opportunity for pupils to work collaboratively on more open-ended tasks, situated within subject activities, as these are most effective in promoting metacognitive understanding. This is because such tasks are more likely to involve pupils in the use of higher-order cognitive interactions, such as reasoning, explaining, debating and so forth, which research (Webb 1985) has shown to be essential for promoting thinking skills and enhancing metacognitive knowledge.

When should teachers intervene?

When making observations in the primary classroom it is not unusual to see teachers direct pupils to start work in their respective groups and then, within a minute of this instruction, begin to circulate around the class either checking that all have understood the task, or giving suggestions or making comments. Galton and Williamson (1992), however, found that when these interventions occurred too early on in the group's deliberations, pupils often saw this as the teacher's attempt to 'take over' and impose his or her views on the group. This was illustrated in the quotation from Chapter 4 where the pupil said 'You no longer feel it's your piece of work' when teachers intervene in this way. Similar sentiments were expressed over a decade later when pupils were questioned on the same issue during the *Spring* Project:

> *Interviewer:*   So are there times when you are in your group when you don't want the teacher to come?
>
> *Fiona:*   Sometimes, but like if we are really stuck, but not at other times.
>
> *Interviewer:*   So if you're not stuck?
>
> *Fiona:*   Mm, no. I don't like it when teachers are on top of you, looking at what you're doing. It gets a bit annoying. Like staring at you.
>
> *Martin:*   Makes you nervous.

Interviewer: So if you are discussing a topic, like today on probability or whatever, and you've got some good ideas and the teacher says 'No'?

Martin: You feel gutted and annoyed and you can't be bothered to work it out again.

Fiona: You feel like, Oh, I've done something wrong. I need to do it again and if it's wrong again you get worked up a bit.

Interviewer: So what should the teacher do?

Martin: Just tell you to rethink your answer.

Fiona: She could give you a clue but you've got to work the rest out on your own.

Interviewer: So, what I'm hearing from you, is that you don't want teachers to interfere too much at the beginning?

Martin: That's right [*other pupils nod in agreement*]. You just want to kind of get off easily at first.

This kind of situation can present teachers with a problem since they often need to scaffold the discussion so that it becomes more focused. In the *Spring* project the Key Stage 3 team worked with teachers to develop a strategy which seemed to work well in these circumstances. Using the argument put forward by Neill (1991) that different areas of the classroom denote different power relationships, the teachers developed the notion of *neutral space*, which was defined as an area of the classroom which belonged to neither the teacher nor the pupils. Thus the space at the front of the class (near the board, OHP, desk, etc.) was where teachers generally engaged in whole-class teaching, with the expectation that any exchanges were under their and not the pupils' direct control. Areas within touching distance of desks or tables belonged to the pupils. However, space at the back of the class, near the door, or by the windows along a side wall belonged to nobody in particular. Teachers then devised the following strategy:

- When first visiting the groups, the teacher signals by means of non-verbal communication (Neill 1991) that he or she is here to listen and not to intervene (for example, some teachers sat with their hand partially over their mouth; others rested their hand on their chin and stood or knelt at right-angles to the table so that their ear rather than mouth was in the pupils' line of vision).

- After a period of listening the teacher goes to one of the areas defined as neutral space and says something along the following lines: 'I've been around the class listening to your discussing in your groups and there are one or two good ideas coming out which you may want to think about and add to your own. I've also had one or two thoughts that you might like to consider ...'

- The teacher is then able to go back to the groups which had difficulties and say: 'Were any of those ideas I talked about a moment ago of any use? What about the one that ...'

It is essential to employ the initial briefing together with the use of non-directive forms of scaffolding (such as the cue cards in the example of the vibration experiment) in support of non-verbal communication strategies of this kind. This ensures that teachers do not have to go around the class endlessly telling groups what they are supposed to be doing because team members have either failed to listen or failed to grasp the initial task directions.

To summarise, the main message of this chapter is that when pupils are trained to work together in groups there are several important outcomes. First, the process promotes *independent thinking*, such that pupils gain a sense of control over their learning. Second, it can develop *speaking and listening skills*, allowing pupils to share feelings and ideas. Third, it can encourage *positive self-esteem*, allowing pupils to build confidence in their own abilities. Fourth it can improve classroom *relationships*, enhancing pupils' sense of social responsibility. Thus group work in classrooms brings pupils together to share information, confront different opinions and to support each other. Teachers may initially feel that it requires a considerable effort on their part if groups are to function effectively. However, the considerable body of research cited in this chapter, and the testimony of teachers who have participated in research such as the *Spring* Project, is evidence that such effort brings its own rewards. As one *Spring* teacher commented, 'I used to think that doing group work was a problem. Now I've come to realise that it's the solution to my problems.'

Key References

Cowie, H., Smith, P., Boulton, M. and Laver, R. (1994) *Cooperation in the Multi-ethnic Classroom*, London: David Fulton.

Dunne, E. and Bennett, N. (1990) *Talking and Learning in Groups*, Basingstoke: Macmillan Education.

Galton, M. and Williamson, J. (1992) *Group Work in the Primary Classroom*, Abingdon: Routledge and Kegan Paul.

Chapter 7

The Social and Emotional Aspects of Teaching and Other Matters

It has long been recognised that most human activity, including both teaching and learning, is not simply a cognitive process but is influenced by other factors, notably the way that individuals feel about themselves. This in turn is strongly influenced by the social environment in which the activity takes places. Andy Hargreaves (2001), for example, argues that emotion and cognition, feeling and thinking, combine together in all social practices in complex ways. In particular, during the past two decades, these aspects of teaching have been driven by the development of research into the concept of emotional intelligence (Day 1998; Goleman 1998). As Hargreaves points out, however, the interpretation of these research findings has been highly individualistic so that judging whether a person is likely to become a committed, warm, caring teacher is seen as a matter of 'personal disposition, moral commitment or private virtue' rather than in terms of criteria that attempt to generalise to all teachers to provide a 'more contextualised view of how emotion sensitises us to the changing context of the specific work life of teaching' (2001: 1057). Hargreaves describes these common dispositions, which all teachers share, as *emotional geographies*. These consist of:

> The spatial and experiential patterns of closeness and distance in human interactions or relationships that help create, configure and colour the feelings and emotions we experience about ourselves, our world and each other. (2001: 1061)

Hargreaves (2000, 2001) lists four main kinds of geographies that characterise teachers' working lives. The first of these is *social cultural*, where differences in culture and class sometimes separate teachers from the parents and pupils. The second concerns a *moral* dimension in which teachers' beliefs are at odds with the policies that they are required to work under, and where no mechanism exists for resolving these differences. There are also *professional* geographies, where the notion of what it is to be a teacher conflicts with the demands of the job, and *political* geographies, where the hierarchical relationship between teachers and policy makers (either within or outside of the school) distorts the understanding of each other's purposes and aims. Finally, and this was previously thought to apply to secondary schools in particular, Hargreaves identifies the existence of *physical* geographies, where infrequency of contact, particularly the reduced time available for informal social exchanges, creates fragmented episodic encounters that distort the relationships between one's professional colleagues as well as between teachers and their pupils. However, in their recent study of workloads in primary schools, Galton and MacBeath (2002) found that a common complaint among the teachers interviewed was that they had no time to talk with colleagues. More importantly, they were denied opportunities to share with the class those 'magic moments' where an unanticipated event, such as birds feeding in the playground, captured the children's interest and imagination. Teachers reflected that in the past such events could have provided the stimulus for a whole afternoon's lessons. One teacher with 20 years' experience told the interviewer:

> It's very hard when children actually start to say something and you feel 'I can't go in that direction. I can't be pulled down that track because I'm moving away from what I've come to talk about.' You've planned this work, put it down in your objectives and you feel you've got to stay on this particular channel. I do feel sad because I would have gone off at a tangent in the past and we would have talked about other things and they would have drawn in their own experiences. (Galton and MacBeath 2002: 40)

In the context of the 'moment by moment' teaching and learning activities, the key elements in the emotional make-up of teachers and their pupils are likely to be the social, cultural and the moral geographies. As was seen in Chapter 2, although teachers attributed much of their current practice to the impact of both professional and political geographies, the actual patterns of discourse taking place in primary classrooms were longstanding and pre-date the introduction of the National Curriculum, the literacy and numeracy hours and the current high-stakes testing regime. It is not always recognised by policy makers, academics and teachers that the world of the classroom is a very different world from those other environments where learning takes place. One obvious example concerns the way in which young children acquire knowledge at home in comparison to school learning. In the home young children learn a great deal by asking questions, and 'Why mummy, why?' has often driven a parent to distraction. But in school the reverse is true as this exchange around the author's lunch table illustrates. In preparation for a lecture on creativity, and looking for an example of some recent classroom innovation to use for illustrative purposes, the author attempted to engage his 9-year-old grandson as follows:

Grandfather: Now tell me, Adam, what interesting questions did you ask the teacher at school today?

Adam: Don't be silly. You don't go to school to ask question. You go to school to answer them.

There are numerous other examples where the context in which the activity takes place makes a considerable difference; play, for example. There have been numerous well-documented studies that testify to the value of imaginative play in the home as a way of developing children's early understanding (Moyles 1989). Yet in school, Galton and Williamson (1992) found that primary pupils often didn't associate play with learning, arguing that it was not the same as doing work. When asked what work was they replied, 'Work is what you do with the teacher.'

As discussed in earlier chapters, one of the most powerful feelings generated in school is the concern felt by pupils about getting things wrong. This starts at a very early age, at the start of formal schooling as indicated by Barrett (1986), who interviewed children during their first weeks in primary school using a series of photographs as a stimulus. Most of the responses were negative, as the following answers illustrate.

Girl pupil: A boy doesn't know what to do. He is sucking his pencil. He cannot do his work. He must tell the teacher.

Boy pupil: I know how to do it. But I don't know how to paint or mix colours properly.

Boy pupil: I didn't like to write when I came to school. I couldn't make a snail. I couldn't draw a picture, it was too hard. I was too little. I feel miserable when I can't do it. I am frightened I might get it wrong. (Barrett 1986: 82)

Galton (1995) has found similar responses in older primary children. These pupils were shown cartoon pictures of a group of children working in a typical classroom. Among the comments were:

Boy pupil: There's no teacher. You are worried if you're getting things wrong.

Girl pupil: The children in the picture are trying to learn how to do somes. They feel nerves and skared in case they get it wrong.

These kinds of reactions can, in extreme cases, give rise to uncooperative behaviour on the part of some pupils, which in turn has emotional consequences for teachers. It has been shown in a previous chapter that one way of reducing these concerns about failure is to scaffold the task in ways that do not lead to pupils becoming dependent on the teachers but which, nevertheless, lower the risk of giving an inappropriate response. In many cases, however, teachers prefer to limit the opportunities for pupils to exhibit disruptive behaviour by choosing 'safe' routine written activities. These usually have to be undertaken in silence, so that the task of monitoring whether the pupils are on task is made easier. Sometimes teachers may use writing activities as a controlling strategy by telling children 'We were going to do a practical activity next lesson but your behaviour is such that we will do some writing instead.' Writing activities are safe because they enable teachers to feel that they are fully in control of the situation. If a pupil has only written five lines when most of the class has completed at least a page, it seems fair for the teacher to assume that this individual has not been working as hard as his or her peers. The teacher therefore feels fully justified when imposing on this particular pupil the punishment of staying in at lunchtime or after school in order to make up for lost time. Given these circumstances teachers will generally brook no argument and will often be deaf to the pupil's protests, even though there may be a genuine reason for child's indifferent performance. However, greater uncertainty surrounds a situation where pupils are engaged on practical tasks, particularly if performed in groups. In this situation, the teacher may have little objective evidence when deciding whether the talk is task related or consists mainly of social 'chit-chat.' Given these circumstances, the teacher can do little more than exhort the group to 'get on with their work' and may be left with the feeling that he or she is not totally in control of events.

No teacher likes to be put in this situation so that considerations about probable behaviour rank high when planning activities that are intended to promote metacognitive wisdom, since the tasks are likely to be more challenging and therefore a potential source of disruption. Questions concerning the control of pupil behaviour are therefore inextricably linked to the forms of control used to regulate pupils' learning. Too often writers on the subject appear to attribute the causes of misbehaviour to the teacher's limitations (poor planning, dull presentation, non-stimulating classroom environment and so on) rather than recognise that however desirable such conditions are they do not in themselves constitute the main determinants of a successful and orderly classroom. As Hargreaves (2001) suggests, the key to good behaviour lies in understanding the 'emotional geographies' that learners and teachers bring with them when entering the classroom, and of finding ways which allow both parties to express their views openly about how they behave or are treated. It then becomes possible to negotiate solutions that have the support of all members of the class and which are more likely to be carried through because of a sense of common ownership between the teacher and pupils (Doddington *et al.* 1999).

Negotiated learning and negotiated behaviour

From the pupils' perspective, the messages relating to learning and to behaviour in many primary classrooms are ambiguous. This is because different rules appear to operate when the class is engaged in regulating their thinking and when they are concerned with regulating their behaviour. Teachers appear to convey to pupils a message that when engaged in learning they are to *think for themselves*, but when the issue is one concerning their behaviour then they should *do as the teacher says*. Yet a moment's thought should quickly establish that while this message is one that is easily understood by a teacher, its implications may not be so clear to the pupils. On many occasions teachers ask questions, as with dialogic teaching, in order to challenge children so that they can develop their ideas. But on other occasions they may also ask questions with the prime purpose of seeing whether certain pupils are paying attention. For those pupils who are not able to distinguish clearly between the two objectives, it is a matter of trying to determine exactly what mood the teacher is in. By far the best strategy for a pupil to adopt in these circumstances, in order to discover what is required on a particular occasion, will be to avoid answering any questions until another pupil has done so.

Concern about pupils' behaviour was identified as the main preoccupation of teachers at secondary level by MacBeath and Galton (2004), but there is some recent evidence that it is also a matter of increasing concern at primary level (MacBeath *et al.* 2006). One frequently adopted approach in dealing with this situation is the package referred to as 'assertive discipline'. In recent years, this approach has gained widespread acceptance in English schools, despite the fact that earlier evidence from the United States shows that such schemes deliver only marginal improvements in behaviour (Emmer and Aussiker 1989). The main objective of such programmes is to create a set of discipline codes for both school and classroom behaviour and attach to these a list of sanctions for those pupils who fail to comply with the code. This list increases in severity as the pupils' offences mount up. Positive encouragement is given in cases where children who in the past have failed to observe the codes come back into line. In some cases, for example, a situation emerges where a pupil who has come off report and maintained the required standards for two weeks is given time out from lessons, while other pupils who have observed the rules all along go unrewarded. Typical of an 'assertive discipline' programme is the policy of a semi-rural primary school shown in Figure 7.1.

Best Behaviour

A summary of the school's behaviour policy for you to read with your child.

Aims

We aim to encourage children to behave in a responsible manner, taking responsibility for their own behaviour so that everyone may enjoy a happy, safe, pleasant environment in which each individual is respected and valued.

Assertive discipline

This is the system used within the school. The staff in the school promotes good behaviour through positive interaction with the children. The children understand the rules, rewards and consequences. The children are rewarded for positive behaviour, if they do not behave there are a fixed set of consequences that members of the school staff adhere to:

Rules

- Follow instructions from any adult working in the school.

- Keep hands and feet to yourself.

- Listen to others when they are speaking.

- Walk inside school.

Rewards

Children will be rewarded for positive behaviour through:

- Verbal praise.

- Stickers or signatures.

- A good note home.

- 5-minutes extra play.

- Headteacher award.

- A good behaviour award.

▶

Figure **7.1** Example of a semi-rural primary school's discipline policy

Consequences

- Verbal warning.

- 2 minutes isolation in the classroom.

- 5 minutes isolation in the classroom.

- 15 minutes working in another classroom.

- Sent to Headteacher or his Deputy with a letter sent to parent/carer.

Codes of conduct

Codes of conduct and discipline plans will be displayed and referred to. Active teaching about behaviour will also take place during circle time, and Personal, Social and Health Education (PSHE) lessons.

Figure **7.1** Example of a semi-rural primary school's discipline policy (continued)

Watkins and Wagner (2000) are of the opinion that 'assertive discipline' packages, such as the above with its 'one size fits all' formula, are unlikely to be a realistic solution to indiscipline given the great variety of pupils' backgrounds in most of today's schools. They argue for a diagnostic view of the conditions leading to a breakdown in behaviour. And, while they agree that assertive discipline can be useful in situations where teachers regularly get involved in long drawn-out confrontations with some pupils, they criticise its all too fre- quent use in an automatic and inflexible manner. More importantly, they argue that although the aim of those who created the assertive discipline approach was to improve communications between teachers and pupils, it is more often used in an attempt to increase compliance. For example, there is a marked inconsistency in the above document which claims in its aims 'to encourage children to take responsibility for their own behaviour', but gives the same children little say about the way in which the stated rules operate. As Watkins and Wagner (2000: 48) also point out, the notion of 'staged responses', where departures from any of the publicised school or classroom rules are responded to by moving to the next stage of response, does not allow discussion of the situation, nor the generation of new solutions jointly by class and teacher, and thus has an important bearing on the nature of the relationship between the two.

The last point is critical to the issue of the ambiguities that often exist between teaching and behaviour, particularly when the purpose of teaching is to create megacognitively-wise students who, if deemed capable of managing their own learning, must surely be capable of applying the same cognitive processes to the management of their behaviour. In both cases it is important to allow pupils to think for themselves, and when they fail to succeed in solving a problem to have opportunities to undertake a review of their situation in order to decide on future action. It seems reasonably clear that the same parameters must operate when the failure to learn is mainly the result of poor behaviour in the classroom.

Thus as a general principle, although clearly there will be particular instances of behaviour which have to be dealt with quickly and firmly because of the way in which they affect others in the class, the same pedagogy used when teaching for understanding and metacognitive wisdom needs also to operate in developing patterns of good behaviour. Watkins and Wagner (2000: 84), following Rogers (1991), argue that classroom rules, as something that cannot be avoided, should be the subject of negotiation. Setting aside time to review the rules and to see whether they're fulfilling their purposes is also essential.

Giving pupils a voice

At the heart of this debate is the wider question of allowing pupils to exercise a voice in the school's deliberations about teaching, learning and other school matters (Rudduck 2003; Rudduck and Flutter 2004). Rudduck points out that this aspiration is central to Citizenship Education and the 1989 United Nations Convention on the Rights of the Child. She quotes a child in the class of a teacher who participated in one of her projects who wrote in her diary:

> 'Sometimes I wish I could sit down with one of my teachers and just tell them what I exactly think about their class. It might be good, it might be bad, and it's just that you don't have the opportunity to do it'. (Webb 2001: 1)

Rudduck (2002) contends that pupils are more likely to do well when they feel more positive about learning and about themselves as learners as a result of pupil consultations. She is supported in this assertion by both Sammons *et al.* (1994) and Gray *et al.* (1999), whose reviews of the teacher effectiveness literature have concluded that schools tended to make greater academic progress where pupils had opportunities to express their views and to exercise a degree of responsibility with respect to the management of the school. Over and above the obvious vehicles for allowing pupils to express their opinions, such as 'circle time' and 'student councils', Rudduck (2003: 85) suggests the use of 'working parties' to explore particular problems and 'message boxes' where pupils can post comments or make suggestions. These procedures should be used sparingly, however, so that pupils don't become blasé about the value attached to their opinions. But of greater importance is the climate in which these various procedures operate. Pupils must feel comfortable in putting forward their views, 'especially if they are acknowledging that they are having difficulties in learning or want the teacher to change his or her approach' (Rudduck 2003: 86).

One example of the success of this approach is described by Galton (1989), where the teacher negotiated a system of sharing out optimum time between the 28 pupils in her class of 9-year-olds. She began by posing her problem to the children after one particularly difficult afternoon when all the pupils seemed to want her attention. She said to the class:

> 'When you all come out like this I don't know what to do and feel very frustrated. I know you want my help and I'm really interested in what you're doing. I want to talk to you about your work but all the time I keep on thinking of the others that are waiting and this makes me try to get through with you as quickly as possible so that I can start on the next pupil. Can you help me to solve this problem?'

After some discussion the children decided to keep a record of the reasons why they came out to see the teacher. Some children were amazingly frank and said, 'I felt bored'. In most cases, however, the reasons had to do with the need to obtain information, to check answers, to receive permission or to spend time talking over their ideas. From this point the teacher and the children went on to decide their respective priorities and to look for alternative solutions which met some of their needs. Certain permissions were dealt with by an agreed set of rules (for example, going to the lavatory). It was also agreed that if more than three people were waiting to see the teacher, then the next pupil would stay back and carry on with work until the number in the queue reduced. Information about a correct answer or a question about what to do next should, whenever possible, be obtained from a neighbour. Other answers should be looked up in the teacher's workbook.

Together, the teacher and the class decided it was more important to provide an extended period of time when pupils could talk over their ideas with the teacher, particularly about their story writing or their art work. A booking system was therefore arranged for a limited period each day, and it was agreed that each pupil could have at least five minutes of this extended time per week. If other pupils needing assistance couldn't get help from their neighbour, they were to go on with something else till the daily extended time session was over.

The system worked well. Observations in the classrooms showed there were higher levels of time on task once the schedule had been put into operation. The schedule was flexible and with the agreement of the class the teacher could increase the time for some pupils, particularly on occasions where special help was needed (Galton 1989: 159).

Should teaching accommodate different learning styles?

In the course of presenting these ideas at various conferences, teachers have raised certain questions. One frequently asked enquiry concerns the relationship of these pedagogic strategies to pupils' learning styles. The notion of learning style has developed out of Howard Gardner's work on multiple intelligences (Gardner 1983, 1999). Initially, Gardner was attracted to the challenge of trying to expand the idea of what it was to be intelligent. In his earlier studies he noticed a tendency for developmental psychologists to use examples from science rather than from the arts as illustrations of higher-order thinking. Gardner and his colleagues therefore began by attempting to trace how children learned to think and perform like artists, in much the same way that Piaget had identified the growth of children's capacity to think like scientists. Much of this work has been done within the context of *Project Zero* at the Harvard Graduate School of Education. Gardner found that most theories of intelligence were concerned with problem solving rather than the creation of products as in art, and therefore sought to widen the definition to include 'an ability to solve problems or create products that are valued within one or more cultural settings' (Gardner 1999: 33). From this expanded definition emerged the theory of *multiple intelligences*, with the central proposition that there were seven separate forms of human intelligence. The first two of these, *linguistic* and *logical mathematical*, are the ones normally tested by traditional intelligence tests. Three of the remaining intelligences are found within the artistic domain and include *musical* intelligence, *bodily kinesthetic* intelligence and *spatial* intelligence. The final two intelligences Gardner called *inter-personal* and *intra-personal* intelligences. The former he defined as 'a person's capacity to understand the intentions, motivation and desires of other people and consequently to work effectively with others', while the latter involved 'the capacity to understand oneself' (Gardner 1999: 43). Intrapersonal intelligence concerns not only an individual's ability to regulate his or her thinking, but also the capacity to control desires, fears and other emotions.

Those that have taken up Gardner's theories have been quick to point out that if the idea of multiple intelligences is valid, then it follows that its different components will be distributed in different ways across the population, as in the case of general intelligence. It then follows, so the argument runs, that learners will respond better if the teaching approach adopted makes recognition of these strengths. Thus, for example, a kinaesthetic person will respond more effectively if, say, data is presented in pictorial form as pie charts rather than in a matrix of numbers. Gardner himself has never endorsed the extension of his theory in this way. He does, as discussed in Chapter 4, suggest that a concept will only be well understood when pupils are able to represent its core features in several ways, but elsewhere he contests the notion that intelligence is the same thing as a learning style, arguing that:

> this assumption needs to be investigated … In my view the relationship between my concept of intelligence and the various conceptions of style need to be worked out empirically on a style-by-style basis. We cannot assume that style means the same thing by all who have used the term, such as psychologists Karl Jung and Jerome Kagan or the educators Tony Gregorc and Bernice McCarthy. Little evidence exists that a person who evinces a style in one milieu or with one content or test will necessarily do so with other diverse contents. And even less basis exists for equating style with intelligence. (Gardner 1999: 84)

In a review for the Learning Skills Council, Coffield *et al.* (2003) has examined the empirical evidence concerning the question of whether the use of learning styles has a positive impact on student learning. In support of the point made by Howard Gardner in the above quotation (concerning the numerous different interpretations of learning style), Coffield and his colleagues were able to identify 71 different models of learning style which they were eventually able to accommodate within five major categories. One major distinction was found between models that viewed an individual's learning style as a 'fixed trait', which was largely biologically determined, and others that represented styles as a repertoire of strategic approaches for tackling specific tasks, but where individuals tended to favour one approach in particular. The consequences for teaching in each case are profound. In using the fixed trait model, teachers would need to diagnose students' learning styles and match the curriculum and the instruction to accommodate these individual preferences. This is no easy task in a class of 30 or more children and Coffield *et al.* (2003) found little evidence that this kind of matching was effective. They quote research which suggests that matching instruction to an individual's preferred style produces relatively small effect sizes (average + 0.14) when resulting attainment is measured. Like Gardner in the above quotation, they also suggest that there is evidence that students may change their learning preferences according to the task and also over time.

For these reasons Coffield and his colleagues endorse the strategic models of learning styles. They suggest that effective teaching should be concerned to encourage an individual to develop the other style traits which do not appear to feature so prominently in that pupil's repertoire. Pupils who find difficulty interpreting a data matrix should be helped to overcome this weakness rather than having the teacher simply replace the numbers with a pictorial representation. This is not to say that graphical images should not be used to reinforce, complement and illustrate the number work. Learning styles should therefore be seen as developmental rather than fixed. The underlying principle behind this application of learning styles is that effective learning is situated within the demands of the task so that pupils therefore need to develop a range of styles for solving different kinds of problems. This alternative approach is much closer to the perspective adopted elsewhere in this book. There it has been argued, for example, that to become metacognitively wise, pupils have to learn the ways scientists, writers and experts in other domains think strategically. The contention is that it is the demands of a particular task that determine how it is best attempted. Pupils may have a preferred way of 'doing things' but this may not always be the best way. While, therefore, the teacher may wish to identify a pupil's preferred learning style, the purpose in doing so will be very different from that employed by those who believe in the 'fixed trait' model. The prime objective will now be to identify the pupils' weaknesses as well as their strengths, so that they can eventually develop a range of adaptive approaches to meet the demands of different tasks. This can be accommodated within the processes of strategic thinking and self-regulation which are key components of becoming metacognitively wise. Learning style inventories can therefore be an important diagnostic tool, in that 'they offer the teacher and pupils a useful vocabulary for discussing the relative merits of using different approaches for meeting the demands of specific tasks, particularly those which are challenging' (Coffield *et al.* 2003: 10). In this respect, pupils with different learning preferences can learn from each other within the context of cooperative group work. In the *Spring* Project, for example, one science teacher formed her groups on the basis of mixed learning styles rather than using attainment scores.

Specific v. generic skill training

A second issue often raised by teachers concerns the various skill training programmes designed to help develop critical thinking, creativity, and so on. The question arises as to how these should be incorporated into the three-part pedagogic model, adopted in this book, where it has been argued that teaching strategic thinking is best done within the context of individual subject disciplines. As discussed in Chapter 5, a review of these thinking skill frameworks by Moseley *et al.* (2005) also put forward a three-part model which is not dissimilar to the one proposed in this book. Their first category was termed 'information gathering', which is analogous to this book's procedural knowledge category. Information gathering involves experiencing, recognising and recording information, and comprehending messages. Moseley *et al.*'s second category was labelled 'building understanding' and again closely resembles this book's second category, conceptual knowledge development.

Building understanding includes the development of meaning by representing or sharing ideas, working with patterns and rules, concept formation and organising ideas. The final strand in the Moseley model, termed 'productive thinking', concerns the ability to reason, understand causal relationships, undertake systematic enquiries, problem solve and think creatively. All the above skills contribute to the kind of strategic thinking that is required for the development of metacognitive knowledge, which is this book's third category. Moseley *et al.*'s classification, however, clearly delineates the higher-cognitive from metacognitive/self-regulatory processes. They acknowledge that there is ambiguity about the separation of these terms but concede that 'both involve strategic and reflective thinking and concern awareness of control, not only of cognitive processes but also of those relating to motivation and affect' (2005: 378).

The differences between the two approaches appear to be one of degree and of terminology. For example, in one Hong Kong P1 classroom the teacher attempted to teach children a quick way of doing addition sums involving the number 9. She wrote on the board the following sums:

$$12 + 9 =$$
$$17 + 9 =$$
$$14 + 9 =$$
$$19 + 9 =$$
$$11 + 9 =$$

The children worked in pairs, each checking the other's calculation, and produced the answers 21, 26, 23, 28 and 20. Most pupils used either their fingers or counters to get these results, and the teacher entered the children's answers on the board with a tick against each sum to indicate that it was correct. She then asked the pupils if they could see a link between the numbers in each sum: 'What do the answers have in common?'

Moseley *et al.* (2005) would regard this episode as an example of 'metacognitive awareness', in that the teacher was attempting to teach the class a quick way of adding 9 to another number. The process could later be extended to other numbers such as 8, 7 and so on. Others might argue, however, that the procedure is little more than a 'memorising' rule for processing information more quickly (similar to a sub-routine in a computer programme), and as such should be taught directly. As such it does not encompass the kinds of strategic thinking required for metacognitive awareness. In practice, the pupils failed to spot the relationship. They told the teacher that the common feature was that each sum had a tick after the answer.

Nevertheless, two important questions arise from Moseley *et al.*'s (2005) analysis. First, if these cognitive processes are to be viewed as a series of increasingly complicated skills, should they be taught directly? Second, should they be included in the curriculum as a distinct 'thinking skills' course? For example, in the case of critical thinking there are a whole range of training programmes such as those developed by Halpern (1998). Students are first taught *verbal reasoning* skills, including the capacity to comprehend and defend a viewpoint against the persuasive techniques that are embedded in everyday language (as in newspapers, television and advertising). The next step involves *argument analysis* skills (identifying one conclusion from a set of statements and one reason that supports that conclusion). Students then go on to *test hypotheses*. This involves learning about scientific procedures, such as predicting and fair-testing. Students, at this stage, might be taught to use scaffolding supports such as mind maps and other techniques for generating hypotheses and thinking 'outside the box'. Next, students explore the different forms of probability (cumulative, exclusive and contingent) in estimating the *likelihood and uncertainty* of certain consequences which may follow a decision. Finally, the above skills are used sequentially to *reach decisions* in solving real-life problems. This stage includes thinking *creatively* because, Halpern (1998: 452) argues, 'of its importance in generating alternatives and restating problems and goals.'

Critics of this approach argue that thinking skills learned in this way are not always easily transferred to other contexts. For this reason it is preferable to integrate the use of these skills within the regular curriculum (Swartz and Parks 1994) rather than offering a separate course that focuses on cognitive processes and not specific content, such as Feuerstein's (1980) well-known enrichment programmes. In the United Kingdom an integrated approach has successfully been used by McGuinness *et al.* (1997, 2000). She argues that this approach is particularly suitable for Key Stage 2 because:

> Thinking skills are matched directly with a topic in the curriculum; content instruction is invigorated thus leading to deeper understanding; classroom time is used optimally; teaching for thoughtfulness is directly supported across the curriculum and transfer of learning can be more easily promoted and reinforced at other stages. (McGuinness 1999: 22)

Halpern, in making the opposite case, argues that 'the Achilles' heel of transfer' is merely a problem of memory training in that 'recognising the need to use a particular skill in a novel context involves the ability of external cues to trigger the retrieval process in the long-term memory', and this is best done through 'meaningful practice with feedback' (1998: 453). However, Halpern readily concedes that the problem in learning to use thinking skills in a variety of different situations is that there are often 'no obvious cues in the novel contexts that can trigger the thinking skills required.' For this reason, therefore, students need to be taught to identify the *structural* features of any problem or situation so that they can recognise similar features in novel situations. Structure *sensitivity* requires students to be able 'to code and manipulate relational knowledge' (Hummel and Holyoak 1997: 427). This is best done by embedding such structures within a web of other related structures, and Halpern argues that in every case the structural aspects of a problem or the main features of an argument should be emphasised. In this way 'they can function as retrieval cues' on future occasions (Halpern 1998: 454).

Too often thinking skills techniques are taught as part of the Personal, Social and Health education (PSHE) course and never practised in the context of the various subject disciplines. As discussed in the previous chapter, training in group work is a case in point. But the opposite approach, teaching thinking skills for use in particular subject contexts, also needs to develop structure sensitivity. In theory, this should be much easier to accomplish in primary schools where the class teacher has control over most of the curriculum. It requires a conscious effort on the part of the teacher to determine what features there are in common across the various disciplines when pupils engage in problem solving, hypothesising, or making judgements about the validity of the evidence and so on. In the primary context this may be best done within the context of topic work.

Ultimately, which approach to use depends on the teacher's core beliefs about learning and teaching. We might speculate that Mrs Clarke in Chapter 1 would opt for a more directly-taught thinking skills approach, while Mr Vincent would be content to explore ways of helping his pupils to acquire metacognitive wisdom across the curriculum by using the teaching principles developed throughout this book. If in the matter of creativity, for example, a teacher accepts the view of the National Advisory Committee on Creative and Cultural Education (1999) that all creative acts involve 'thinking or behaving *imaginatively* through *purposeful activity* to generate an *original* outcome which must have *value*', then a programme such as that devised by Halpern (2002) will appeal. Pupils will be taught to redefine a problem in several different ways; find analogies across several knowledge domains; list relevant terms; brainstorm; generate a list of ways in which a particular solution can vary; list positive, negative and interesting attributes of different solutions, and visualise their chosen solution from other perspectives. If, on the other hand, the view is taken that the act of creation is more than its component parts, then the definition offered by the theatre director Jude Kelly (NUT/NCA 2002: 40) that it merely requires 'athleticism of the mind' will find favour, and Halpern's programme is unlikely to appeal. As an artist, Kelly's position is consistent with Howard Gardner's observation that many cognitive enrichment programmes reflect a bias towards scientific thinking: certainly this is true in the case of Halpern's interpretation of what it means to 'think critically'. Teachers who are sympathetic to Kelly's viewpoint are therefore more likely to believe that teaching pupils to be metacognitively wise will be sufficient to ensure that the work they produce will often be both imaginative and original. In this sense, creativity is about pupils feeling comfortable with the notion that the mind can reshape ideas and creative teaching is about unlocking this potential in the ways described in previous chapters.

Personalised learning or personalised schooling?

This book began by expressing a degree of scepticism about Professor Michael Barber's claim that under New Labour the teaching profession had finally reached the age of *informed professionalism*. There is, of course, nothing wrong with the idea of informed professionals, provided teachers are free to make their own judgements about the quality of the evidence on offer. They also require the freedom to interpret such evidence in ways that match the needs of the children they teach, rather than face criticism because much of their lesson has not been taught within a whole-class framework. There are welcome signs that many teachers are now willing to take the risk of making these decisions for themselves rather than responding to the dictates of government. But the challenges are great, not least because there is now a whole generation of teachers who entered primary schools in the 1980s and who have only experience of the National Curriculum to fall back on. They have been trained as teachers to implement the literacy and numeracy strategies and have spent their entire careers attempting to discharge this task to the satisfaction of the Ofsted inspectors.

When these teachers ask how they can break out of the existing culture it seems sensible to suggest that they should start in small ways by, for example, 'being subversive on Fridays'. The argument is that attempting something new on a Monday would be likely to end up as the main talking point in the staff room for the rest of the week, particularly if it did not go well on the first occasion. But if something new was done on a Friday, the talk at Monday morning's coffee break will mainly consist of the weekend's personal triumphs and disasters.

Of course, in an ideal world, free of the pressures of excessive testing and the use of such tests for accountability purposes, there would be no need for teachers to face the dilemma of teaching in ways that satisfied Government demands, while at the same time recognising that what was being taught neither stimulated pupils nor adequately equipped them to cope with the uncertainties of the 21st century. As one teacher expressed it in Galton and MacBeath's study of primary teachers' working lives:

> I would like less pressure to achieve results and more freedom to develop each child's full potential, to stimulate their curiosity, harness their energy, develop them as individuals and members of a community. (2002: 45)

The most recent government initiative, which it is claimed has been devised to meet this teacher's concerns, is *personalised learning*, since it is designed to make 'every young person's learning experience stretching, creative, fun and successful' (DfES 2004: 3). This term first surfaced as part of Tony Blair's speech to the Labour Party Conference in 2003 when it was said to be about 'putting citizens at the heart of public services'. It was taken up by an education minister, David Miliband, at the North of England Conference in January 2004. For Miliband, the concept involved 'high expectations of every child, given practical form by high-quality teaching based on a sound knowledge and understanding of every child's needs'. Little clarification how schools were to engage in this task emerged from the subsequent government White Paper, *Higher Standards, Better Schools For All*, with the sub-title, *More Choice for Parents and Pupils* (DfES 2005). Chapter 4, devoted to the topic of personalised learning, suggests that the system should focus on the 'needs of the individual child' with 'intensive small group tuition in literacy and numeracy for those falling behind, including one-to-one support where appropriate and extra stretch for the gifted and talented' (DfES 2005: para. 4.6). There is also a subtle shift in the same paragraph where the term 'interactive' has been replaced by 'excellent tailored' whole-class teaching as the recommended pedagogy, although what this entails is not explicated. Neither do the examples provided in the chapter offer further clarification. Helping children who have fallen behind appears to involve 'more of the same' and consists of organising training in literacy and numeracy for teachers, booster classes for Years 1 and 2 pupils, and courses for parents (some accredited by the local FE College) in supporting the children's reading at home. Flexibility in the curriculum allows more gifted secondary pupils to do the Key Stage National Tests at the end of Year 8, thus starting GCSEs a year earlier, and setting by ability is put forward as the 'recommended' way of 'providing each child with a tailored education' (2005: para. 437). The latter point is particularly interesting in that the White Paper refers to 'shortly to be published' research to support this view, although the actual research

(Kutnick *et al.* 2005) and its follow-up (Kutnick *et al.* 2006) comes to the conclusion that there is no unequivocal evidence that setting raises achievement.

The supporting document provided by the Standards Unit, *A National Conversation about Personalised Learning*, defines the five key components of a personalised approach: assessment for learning; effective teaching and learning strategies; curriculum entitlement and choice; school organisation; and strong partnerships beyond the school (DfES 2004: 8–14). The latter category includes parental and community participation, coordinated action with other services (Health and Social Care) and partnerships with the business community. The section on the second key component, 'Effective Teaching and Learning Strategies', consists of two short paragraphs of a vague and extremely general kind. Teachers should employ strategies that 'develop the competence and confidence of every learner by actively engaging and stretching them' and make use of a range of 'whole class, group and individual teaching, learning and ICT strategies to transmit knowledge, to instil key learning skills and to accommodate different paces of learning' (DfES 2004: 9).

A document produced by the DfES Standards Unit with the title, *A Conversation about Personalised Learning* claims in its introductory paragraph that 'the idea [of personalised learning] is capturing the imagination of teachers and children' (White 2006). However, a recent and as yet unpublished survey, carried out by the author and his colleague, Susan Steward, on behalf of the DfES, would suggest that actual response by schools to the personalised learning initiative is one of confusion and uncertainty as to its purposes and the implications in practical terms for current classroom practice. Over three-quarters of schools claimed that they were putting personalised learning into practice through a variety of ways. These included assessment for learning; targeted interventions; special topic days; enrichment for all; curriculum choice; behavioural policies and giving pupils 'a voice' in school policy making. However, when asked if these various interventions were introduced specifically in response to the personalised learning initiative, over 80 per cent of schools responded negatively. Primary schools identified a number of features designed to improve teaching and learning. These included thinking skills training, the use of the programme Philosophy for Children (Fisher, 1998; Lipman *et al.* 1980), various applications of learning styles, brain gym and the use of interactive whiteboards. But less than 4 per cent of respondents stated that they had introduced ability grouping as a response to personalised learning in line with the DfES recommendation. It appeared that in most cases schools had 'tweaked' existing practice rather than introduced new initiatives.

In primary schools confusion appeared to centre on the government pronouncement that personalised learning was not intended to re-introduce the 'individualised, child-centred' approaches of the Plowden era. According to John White, the philosopher of education, this confusion is not surprising since it suits the interests of politicians 'to gloss things over'. This is because 'rhetorical language is part of their armoury', unlike teachers 'who don't have an interest in fuzzy language since their job demands that they be as clear as they can about what they are doing.' For politicians, on the other hand, 'over-generality pays dividends' because, for example, while everyone is in favour of meeting children's needs, being specific and suggesting that extra resources should be given to the SEN sector at the expense of other budgets may mean that 'you risk losing supporters' (White 2006). White's summarises his view with the following observation:

> What personalised learning is I really don't know. I don't mean by this that it's all as yet
> something of a mystery, or that, as official bodies like to put it these days, the concept is still
> 'evolving, and 'emergent'. I would prefer to say that the linguistic rot that Miliband and the
> DfES started is still continuing.

> Many of the ideas that have affixed themselves to the term make good sense ... Pupils
> should have more opportunities to participate in the assessment of their work collectively as
> well as individually. Teaching *should* be responsive to the differing motivation of learners.
> The school curriculum does need to get away from the stranglehold of discrete subjects and
> equip learners to lead a flourishing personal and civic life ... I would be the first to agree that
> these statements need to be explicated further ... Plain language helps chart the way ahead.
> 'Personalised learning' and the jargon it has generated just gets in the way. (2006)

The Teaching and Learning Research Programme (TLRP) has attempted to take up White's
challenge by looking at various individual research projects within the programme that have
a bearing on the five key components which the DfES claims define the idea of personalised
learning. For example, the *Learning How to Learn Project* emphasises the use of Assessment for
Learning (AfL), but has found that only about one-fifth of the teachers involved were able to
use assessment in ways that promoted pupil autonomy as the principles of (AfL) require.
This was despite nearly all participating teachers reporting that these principles were in
'broad alignment with their personal values'. The researchers concluded that:

> Personalised learning is not a matter of tailoring the curriculum, teaching and assessment to fit
> the individual but a question of developing social practices that enable people to become all
> that they are capable of becoming ... AfL can sometimes be taken on at a superficial level
> without the deeper changes in practices and relationships which actually affect the outcomes.
> (TLRP 2006: 7)

Elsewhere in the document there is a description of the use of information and communication technology (ICT) to promote key mathematical ideas. The teacher reported that
while he began by following the literacy hour structure, this became increasingly difficult as
the pupils became more involved. The researchers add that the lesson was 'a timely
reminder that learning doesn't happen in straight lines' but 'is a social and shared experience which at times can appear chaotic, and fragmented as we share ideas and try them out'
(TLRP 2006: 18). In their concluding remarks they argue that:

> If Personalised Learning is to become synonymous with individualised learning, this is likely
> to limit the knowledge creation of future generations of citizens. If personalisation becomes
> linked to communities of learning and partnerships between teachers, parents and young
> people then we will be building a solid base for educating young people for the 21st century.
> (TLRP 2006: 18–19)

Thus it is *personalised schooling* rather than personalised learning that should be the goal.

As with classrooms, where it has been argued throughout this book that teachers have to adjust the broad principles governing teaching and learning to meet the particular contexts of their classroom, so the same is true of schools. At the heart of the comprehensive ideal is the need for each school to balance the provision of 'equality of opportunity' for all its students with the need to develop each pupil's 'full potential'. Where to set this balance must be influenced, in part, by the local environment in which each school operates, and not solely by the dictates of national policy. But if the outcomes of such deliberations are to satisfy all 'stakeholders' (teachers, parents, students, local businesses and so on) as the government claims it intends under its drive to put the 'citizen at the centre of public services', then schools must have the freedom to work things out for themselves within the confines of less rigid frameworks of national accountability and testing than currently operate. Only then will schools be able, with confidence, to create the kind of learning communities advocated by Watkins (2005: 196) and others where 'the challenge is to create a proactive culture in the classroom' that while it may not 'reflect some aspects of the surrounding culture [can] act as a model of what the surrounding culture might become' (2005: 196). This book, hopefully, makes a modest contribution to this 'brave new world'.

Key references

Hargreaves, A. (2001) Emotional geographies of teaching, *Teachers College Record*, 103(6): 1056–80.

Rudduck, J. and Flutter, J. (2004) *How to Improve Your School: Giving Pupils a Voice*, London: Continuum.

Watkins, C. (2005) *Classrooms as Learning Communities: What's in it for Schools?* Abingdon: Routledge.

References

Ainscow, M. and Tweddle, D. (1984) *Early Learning Skills Analysis*, Chichester: Wiley.

Alexander, P. (2004) The development of expertise: the journey from acclimatisation to proficiency, *Educational Researcher*, 32 (8):10–14.

Alexander, P., Schallert, D. and Hare, V. (1991) Coming to terms: how researchers in learning and literacy talk about knowledge, *Review of Educational Research*, 61(3): 315–43.

Alexander, R. (1992) *Policy and Practice in Primary Education*, Abingdon: Routledge.

Alexander, R. (1995) *Versions of Primary Education*, Abingdon: Routledge.

Alexander, R. (2000) *Culture and Pedagogy: International Comparisons of Primary Education*, Oxford: Blackwell.

Alexander, R. (2004) Still no pedagogy? Principle, pragmatism and compliance in primary education, *Cambridge Journal of Education*, 34 (1): 7–33.

Alexander, R. (2005) *Towards Dialogic Teaching: Rethinking Classroom Talk* 2nd edn, York: Dialogues.

Alexander, R., Willcocks, J. and Kinder, K. (1989) *Changing Primary Practice*, Abingdon: Falmer.

Allport, G. (1966) Expressive behaviour, in Semeonoff, B. (ed.) *Personality Assessment*, London: Penguin.

Alton-Lee, A. and Nuthall, G. (1992) A generative methodology for classroom research, *Educational Philosophy and Theory*, Special Issue: Educational Research Methodology, 24 (2): 29–55.

Alton-Lee, A. and Nuthall, G. (1998) *Inclusive Instructional Design: Theoretical Principles Arising from the Understanding Learning and Teaching Project*, Report to the Ministry of Education, Understanding Learning and Teaching Project 3, Wellington, NZ: Ministry of Education.

Anderson, H. (1939) The measurement of domination and of socially integrative behaviour in teachers' contacts with children, *Child Development*, 10, 73–89.

Anderson, L. and Burns, R. (1989) *Research in Classrooms: The Study of Teachers, Teaching and Instruction*, Oxford: Pergamon.

Anderson, L., Everston, C. and Brophy, J. (1979) An experimental study of effective teaching in first grade reading groups, *Elementary School Journal*, 79: 193–223.

ARG (Assessment Reform Group) (1999) *Assessment for Learning: Beyond the Black Box*, Cambridge: School of Education, University of Cambridge.

Aronson, E. and Patnoe, S. (1997) *The Jigsaw Classroom: Building Cooperation in the Classroom*, Harlow: Longman.

Atkinson, J. (1964) *An Introduction to Motivation*, Princeton, NJ: Van Nostrand.

Atkinson, R. and Shiffrin, R. (1968) Human memory: a proposed system and its control processes, in Spence, J. and Spence, J. (eds) *Advances in the Psychology of Learning and Motivation*, Volume 2, New York: Academic Press.

Atkinson, T. (2000) Learning to teach: intuitive skills and reasoned objectivity, in Atkinson, T. and Claxton, G. (eds) *The Intuitive Practitioner: On the Value of not always Knowing what one is Doing*, Buckingham: Open University Press.

Baines, E., Blatchford, P. and Kutnick, P. (2003) Changes in grouping practice over primary and secondary schools, *International Journal of Educational Research*, 39 (1): 9–34.

Barber, M. (2002) *The Next Stage for Large Scale Reform in England: From Good to Great*, Background Paper presented to the Federal Reserve Bank of Boston 47th Economic Conference, 'Education in the 21st Century: Meeting the Challenges of a Changing World', 19–21 June.

Barker Lunn, J. (1984) Junior School teachers: Their methods and practices, *Educational Research* 26: 178–88.

Barrett, G. (1986) *Starting School: An Evaluation of the Experience*, Final Report to the AMMA, CARE, University of East Anglia.

Beard, R. (1998) *National Literacy Strategy: A Review of the Research and Other Evidence*, London: DfES.

Bee, R. and Bee, F. (1997) *Project Management: The People Challenge*, London: Institute of Personnel and Development.

Benner, P. (1984) *From Novice to Expert: Excellence and Power in Clinical Nursing Practice*, Reading, MA: Addison Wesley.

Bennett, N., Desforges, C., Cockburn, A. and Wilkinson, B. (1984) *The Quality of Pupil Learning Experience*, London: Lawrence Erlbaum.

Bennett, N. and Dunne, E. (1992) *Managing Classroom Groups*, Hemel Hempstead: Simon and Schuster Education.

Bennett, N. and Kell, J. (1989) *A Good Start: Four-year-olds in Infant Schools*, Oxford: Blackwell.

Bentley, T. (1998) *Learning Beyond the Classroom: Education for a Changing World*, Abingdon: Routledge.

Bereiter, C. (1991) Implications of connectionism for thinking about rules, *Educational Researcher*, 27 (2): 4–13.

Bereiter, C. and Scardamalia, M. (1993) *Surpassing Ourselves: An Enquiry into the Nature and Implications of Expertise*, Chicago, IL: Open Court.

Berliner, D. (1994) Expertise: The wonders of exemplary performance, in Mangieri, J. and Collins-Block, C. (eds), *Creating Powerful Thinking in Teachers and Students*, Ft. Worth, TX: Holt, Rinehart and Winston.

Berliner, D. (2002) Learning about and learning from expert teachers, *International Journal of Educational Research*, 37 (6): 463–82.

Berliner, W. (2004) Heaven knows why they are miserable now, *Guardian*, 27 April, p. 2.

Bierhoff, H. and Prais, S. (1995) *Schooling as Preparation for Life and Work in Switzerland and Britain*, Discussion Paper no. 75, London: National Institute of Economic and Social Research.

Biggs, J. (1994) What are effective schools? Lessons from East to West, *Australian Educational Researcher*, 21: 19–40.

Biggs, J. and Collis, K. (1982) *Evaluating the Quality of Learning: The SOLO (Structure of Observed Learning Outcome)*, San Diego, CA: Academic Press.

Black, P. and Wiliam, D. (1998a) Assessment and classroom learning, *Assessment in Education*, 5 (1): 7–75.

Black, P. and Wiliam, D. (1988b) *Inside the Black Box: Raising Standards through Classroom Assessment*, London: King's College, University of London.

Black, P., Harrison, C., Lee, C., Marshall, B. and Wiliam, D. (2003) *Assessment for Learning: Putting it into Practice*, Maidenhead: Open University Press/McGraw-Hill.

Blatchford, P., Kutnick, P., Galton, M. and Baines, E. (2005) *Improving the Effectiveness of Pupil Groups in Classrooms*, A Phase 2 TLRP project, Final Report to the Economic and Social Research Council (ESRC) available at http://creict.homerton.cam.ac.uk/spring

Bliss, T., Robinson, G. and Maines, B. (1995) *Developing Circle Time*, London: Lame Duck.

Block, J. (1971) *Mastery Learning: Theory and Practice*, New York: Holt, Rinehart and Winston.

Bloom, B. (1976) *Human Characteristics and School Learning*, New York: McGraw-Hill.

Bransford, J., Brown, A. and Cocking, R. (eds) (1999) *How People Learn: Brain, Mind, Experience and School*, Washington, DC: National Academy Press.

Bredo, E. (1997) The social construction of learning, in Phye, G. (ed.) *Handbook of Academic Learning: Construction of Knowledge*, New York: Academic Press.

Brehony, K. (2005) Primary schooling under New Labour, *Oxford Review of Education*, 31 (1): 29–46.

Brinton, B., Fujiki, M. and Higbee, J. (1998) Participation in cooperative learning activities by children with specific language impairment, *Journal of Speech, Language and Hearing Research*, 41, 1193–206.

Brophy, J. (1992) Probing the subtleties of subject-matter teaching, *Educational Leadership*, 49 (7): 4–8.

Brophy, J. (2004) *Motivating Students to Learn* 2nd edn, Mahwah, NJ: Lawrence Erlbaum.

Brophy, J.E. and Good, T.L. (1986) Teacher behaviour and student achievement, in Wittrock, M. C. (ed.) *Handbook of Research on Teaching* 3rd edn, New York: Macmillan.

Brown, A. (1997) Transforming schools into communities of thinking and learning about serious matters, *American Psychologist*, 52 (4): 399–413.

Brown, A. and Campione, J. (1990) Communities of learning and thinking, or a context by any other name, in Kuhn, D. (ed.) *Developmental Perspectives on Teaching and Learning Thinking Skills: Contributions in Human Development*, pp. 108–26, Basel, Krager.

Brown, A. and Campione, J. (1994) Guided discovery in a community of learners, in McGilly, K. (ed.) *Classroom Lessons: Integrating Cognitive Theory and Classroom Practice*, Cambridge, MA: MIT Press in association with Bradford Books.

Brown, A. and Palincsar, A. (1986) *Guided Cooperative Learning and Individual Knowledge Acquisition*, Technical Report 372, Cambridge, MA: Bolt, Beranak and Newham.

Brown, M., Askew, M., Baker, D., Denvir, H. and Millett, A. (1998) Is the national numeracy strategy research based?, *British Journal of Educational Studies*, 46: 362–85.

Brown, M., Askew, M., Millet, A. and Rhodes, V. (2003) The key role of educational research in the development and education of the National Numeracy Strategy, *British Educational Research Journal*, 29(5): 655–72.

Bruner, J. (1966) *Towards a Theory of Instruction*, Cambridge, MA: Harvard University Press.

Bruner, J. and Clinchy, B. (1972) Towards a disciplined intuition, in Bruner, J. (ed.) *The Relevance of Education*, London: George Allen and Unwin.

Budd-Rowe, M. (1973) *Teaching Science as a Continuous Enquiry*, New York: McGraw-Hill.

Campbell, J. (1998) Broader thinking about the primary school curriculum, in *Take Care, Mr Blunkett*, London: Association of Teachers and Lecturers (ATL).

Carroll, J. (1963) A model for school learning, *Teachers College Record*, 64, 723–33.

Cavendish, S., Galton, M., Hargreaves, L. and Harlen, W. (1990) *Assessing Science in the Primary Classroom: Observing Activities*, London: Paul Chapman Publishing.

CFAS (2003) *School Sampling Project Curriculum Survey: Summary of Primary School Findings, 2001–02*, www.education.man.ac.uk/cfas/mcd/summaries.html. Centre for Formative Assessment Studies

Chitty, C. (2004) *Education Policy in Great Britain*, Basingstoke: Macmillan.

Clariana, R., Wagner, D. and Roher-Murphy, L. (2000) Applying a connectionist description of feedback timing, *Educational Teaching Research and Development*, 48 (3): 5–21.

Claxton, G. (2000) The anatomy of intuition, in Atkinson, T. and Claxton, G. (eds) *The Intuitive Practitioner: On the Value of not always Knowing what one is Doing*, Buckingham: Open University Press.

Coffield, F., Ecclestone, K., Hall, E. and Moseley, D. (2003) *Learning Styles in Learning to Learn: A Review*, Paper Prepared for the ESRC 'Learning to Learn' Seminar, 17 November , London: British Psychological Society.

Cohen, E. (1994) Restructuring classrooms: conditions for productive groups, *Review of Educational Research*, 64 (1): 1–35.

Cohen, E. and Lotan, R. (1995) Producing equal status interaction in the heterogeneous classroom, *American Educational Research Journal*, 32, (1): 99–120.

Conner, C. (2003) What leaders need to know about the relationship between teaching and learning, in *Learning Texts*, Nottingham: National College for School Leadership (NCSL).

Coopersmith, S. (1967) *The Antecedents of Self-esteem*, San Francisco, CA: Freeman.

Cortazzi, M. (1991) *Primary Teaching: How It Is*, London: David Fulton.

Cortazzi, M. (1998) Primary curricula across cultures: contexts and connections, in Moyles, J. and Hargreaves, L. (eds) *The Primary Curriculum: Learning from International Perspectives*, Abingdon: Routledge.

Cortazzi, M. and Jin, L. (1996) Cultures of learning; language classrooms in China, in Coleman, H. (ed.) *Society and Language Classroom*, Cambridge: Cambridge University Press.

Covington, M. (1992) *Making the Grade: A Self-worth Perspective on Motivation and School Reform*, Cambridge: Cambridge University Press.

Cowie, H. and Rudduck, J. (1991) *Cooperative Group Work: Training Guide*, London: BP Educational Service.

Cowie, H., Smith, P., Boulton, M. and Laver, R. (1994) *Cooperation in the Multi-ethnic Classroom*, London: David Fulton.

Csikszentmihalyi, M (1975) *Beyond Boredom and Anxiety*, San Francisco, CA: Jossey-Bass.

Csikszentmihalyi, M. (1990) *Flow: The Psychology of Optimal Experience*, New York: Harper and Row.

Dainton, S. (1998) Introduction, in *Take Care, Mr Blunkett*, London: Association of Teachers and Lecturers (ATL).

Daniels, H. (1994) *Literature Circles: Voice and Choice in the Student-Centred Classroom*, York: Stenhouse.

Daniels, H. (2001) *Vygotsky and Pedagogy*, Abingdon: RoutledgeFalmer.

Dawes, L., Mercer, N. and Wegerif, G. (2000) *Thinking Together: A Programme of Activities for Developing Thinking Skills at Key Stage 2*, Birmingham: Questions Publishing.

Day, C. (1998) *Developing Teachers: The Challenges of Lifelong Learning?*, Abingdon: Falmer.

Delin, C. and Baumeister, R. (1994) Praise, more than just social reinforcement, *Journal for the Theory of Social Behaviour*, 24: 219–41.

Denham, C. and Liberman, A. (eds) (1986) *Time to Learn*, Report of the Beginning Teacher Education Studies, Washington, DC: National Institute of Education.

Desforges, C. (ed.) (1995) *An Introduction to Teaching: Psychological Perspectives*, Oxford: Blackwell.

Desforges, C. (2003) On learning and teaching, in *Learning Texts*, Nottingham: National College for School Leadership (NCSL) at www.ncsl.org.uk

DfEE (1997) *Excellence in Schools*, Cmnd 3681, London: The Stationery Office.

DfEE (1999) *Excellence in Cities*, London: The Stationery Office.

DfES (2003) *Excellence and Enjoyment: A Strategy for Primary Schools*, London: Department for Education and Skills.

DfES (2004) *A National Conversation about Personalised Learning* (DfES/0919/2004), Nottingham: Department for Education and Skills or at www.standards.dfes.gov.uk/personalisedlearning

DfES (2005) *Higher Standards, Better Schools for All: More Choice for Parents and Pupils* (Cm 6677), London: Department for Education and Skills.

Dillon, J. (1990) *The Practice of Questioning*, Abingdon: Routledge.

Doddington, C., Flutter, J. and Rudduck, J. (1999) Exploring and explaining 'dips' in motivation and performance in primary and secondary schooling, *Research in Education*, 61: 29–38.

Doyle, W. (1979a) Classroom tasks and student abilities, in Peterson, P. and Walberg, H. (eds) *Research on Teaching*, Berkeley, CA: McCutchan.

Doyle, W. (1979b) Making managerial decisions in classrooms, in Duke, D. (ed.) *Classroom Management, 78th Yearbook of the National Society for the Study of Education, Part II*, Chicago, IL: University of Chicago Press.

Doyle, W. (1983) Academic work, *Review of Educational Research*, 53: 159–99.

Doyle, W. (1986) Classroom organisation and management, in Wittrock, M. (ed.) *3rd Handbook of Research on Teaching*, New York: Macmillan.

Doyle, W. and Carter, K. (1983) Academic tasks in classrooms, *Curriculum Inquiry*, 14: 129–49.

Dunkin, M. and Biddle, B. (1974) *The Study of Teaching*, New York: Holt, Rinehart and Winston.

Dunne, E. and Bennett, N. (1990) *Talking and Learning in Groups*, Basingstoke: MacMillan Education.

Dweck, C. (1986) Motivational approaches effecting learning, *American Psychologist*, 41, 1040–8.

Dweck, C. and Leggett, E. (1988) A social-cognitive approach to motivation and personality, *Psychological Review*, 95, 256–73.

Earl, L., Levin, B., Leithwood, K., Fullan, M. and Watson, N. (2001) *Watching and Learning 2: OISE/UT Evaluation of the Implementation of the National Literacy and Numeracy Strategies*, Nottingham: DfEE Publications and Toronto: Ontario Institute for Studies in Education, University of Toronto.

Earl, L., Watson, N., Levin, B., Leithwood, K. and Fullan, M. (2003) *Watching and Learning 3: Final Report of the External Evaluation of the Implementation of the National Literacy and Numeracy Strategies*, Nottingham: DfEE Publications and Toronto: Ontario Institute for Studies in Education, University of Toronto.

Earl, L., Fullan, M., Leithwood, K., Watson, N., Jantzi, D., Levin, B. and Torrance, N. (2000) *Watching and Learning 1: OISE/UT Evaluation of the Implementation of the National Literacy and Numeracy Strategies*, Nottingham: DfEE Publications and Toronto: Ontario Institute for Studies in Education, University of Toronto.

Earley, P., Northcroft, G., Lee, C. and Lituchy, T. (1990) Impact of process and outcome feedback on the relation of goal setting to task performance, *Academy of Management Journal*, 33 (1): 87–105.

Edwards, D. and Mercer, N. (1987) *Common Knowledge and the Development of Understanding in the Classroom*, Abingdon: Routledge.

Elliott, J. (1976) *Developing Hypotheses about Classrooms for Teachers: An Account of the Work of the Ford Teaching Project*, Grand Forks, ND: University of North Dakota.

Emmer, E. and Aussiker, A. (1989) School and classroom discipline programs: how well do they work?, in Moles, O. (ed.) *Strategies to Reduce Student Misbehaviour*, Washington, DC: US Department of Education.

Entwistle, N.J. (1977) Strategies of learning and studying: recent research findings, *British Journal of Educational Studies*, 25, 225–38.

Entwistle, N. and Smith, C. (2002) Personal understanding and target understanding: mapping influences on the outcomes of learning, *British Journal of Educational Psychology*, 72 (3): 321–42.

Entwistle, N.J., Hanley, M. and Hounsell, D. (1979) Identifying distinctive approaches to studying, *Higher Education*, 8, 365–80.

Ericsson, K.A. (1996). The acquisition of expert performance: An introduction to some of the issues, in K. A. Ericsson (Ed.), *The Road to Excellence: The Acquisition of Expert Performance in the Arts and Sciences Sports and Games*, Mahwah, NJ: Lawrence Erlbaum, pp. 1–50.

Everton, T., Galton, M. and Pell, T. (2002) Educational research and the teacher, *Research Papers in Education*, 17 (4): 373–401.

Feuerstein, R. (1980) *Instrumental Enrichment Intervention Programme for Cognitive Modifiability*, Baltimore, MD: University Park Press.

Fisher, R. (1998) *Teaching Thinking*, London: Cassell.

Flanders, N.A. (1964) Some relationships among teacher influence, pupil attitudes and achievement, in Biddle, B. and Ellena, W. (eds) *Contemporary Research on Teacher Effectiveness*, New York: Holt, Rinehart and Winston.

Flanders, N. (1970) *Analysing Teacher Behaviour*, Reading, MA: Addison-Wesley.

Fullan, M. (2001) *The New Meaning of Educational Change* 3rd edn, New York: Teachers College Press, Columbia University.

Furlong, J. (2000) Intuition and the crisis in teacher professionalism, in Atkinson, T. and Claxton, G. (eds) *The Intuitive Practitioner: On the Value of not always Knowing what one is Doing*, Buckingham: Open University Press.

Gage, N. (1978) *The Scientific Basis for the Art of Teaching*, New York: Teachers College Press.

Galloway, D., Rogers, C., Armstrong, D., Leo, E. with Jackson, C. (2004) Understanding motivation, in Daniels, H. and Edwards, A. (eds) *The RoutledgeFalmer Reader in Psychology of Education*, Abingdon, RoutledgeFalmer, pp. 89–105.

Galton, M. (1981) Teaching groups in the junior school, a neglected art, *Schools Organisation*, 1 (2): 175–81.

Galton, M. (1989) *Teaching in the Primary School*, London: David Fulton.

Galton, M. (1995) *Crisis in the Primary Classroom*, London: David Fulton.

Galton, M. and Fogelman, K. (1998) The use of discretionary time in the primary school, *Research Papers in Education*, 13: 119–39.

Galton, M. and MacBeath, J. with Page, C. and Steward, S. (2002) *A Life in Teaching? The Impact of Change on Primary Teachers' Working Lives*, A report commissioned by the National Union of Teachers concerning the workloads in Primary Schools, University of Cambridge: Faculty of Education.

Galton, M. and Williamson, J. (1992) *Group Work in the Primary Classroom*, Abingdon: Routledge.

Galton, M., Gray, J. and Rudduck, J. (2003) *Transfer and Transitions in the Middle Years of Schooling (7–14): Continuities and Discontinuities in Learning*, Research Report 443, Nottingham: Department for Education and Skills (DfES).

Galton, M., Hargreaves, L., Comber, C. and Wall, D. (1999) *Inside the Primary Classroom: 20 Years On*, Abingdon: Routledge.

Galton, M., Simon, B. and Croll, P. (1980) *Inside the Primary Classroom*, Abingdon: Routledge and Kegan Paul.

Gardner, H. (1983) *Frames of Mind: The Theory of Multiple Intelligences*, New York: Basic Books.

Gardner, H. (1995) Why would anyone become an expert?, *American Psychologist*, 50: 802–3.

Gardner, H. (1999) *Intelligence Reframed: Multiple Intelligences for the 21st Century*, New York: Basic Books.

Gardner, H. and Boix-Mansilla, V. (1994) Teaching for understanding in the disciplines and beyond, *Teachers College Record*, 96 (2): 198–217.

Gipps, C. (1994) *Beyond Testing: Towards a Theory of Educational Assessment*, Abingdon: Falmer.

Glaser, R. (1987) Thoughts on expertise, in Schooler, C. and Schaie, W. (eds) *Cognitive Functioning and Social Structure over the Life Course*, Norwood, NJ: Ablex.

Glaser, R. (1990) Expertise, in Eysenk, M., Ellis, A., Hunt, E. and Johnson-Laird, P. (eds), *The Blackwell Dictionary of Cognitive Psychology*. Oxford: Blackwell Reference.

Glaser, R. (1996) Changing the agency for learning: Acquiring expert performance, in Ericsson, K. (ed.) *The Road to Excellence: The Acquisition of Expert Performance in the Arts and Sciences, Sports and Games* Mahwah, NJ: Lawrence Erlbaum, pp. 303–11.

Goleman, D. (1998) *Working with Emotional Intelligence*, New York: Bantham.

Good, C. (1973) *Dictionary of Education* 3rd edn., New York: McGraw-Hill.

Good, T. and Brophy, J. (2002) *Looking in the Classroom* 9th edn, Boston, MD: Allyn and Bacon.

Good, T. and Grouws, D. (1979) The Missouri mathematics effectiveness project: an experimental study of fourth grade classrooms, *Journal of Educational Psychology*, 71 (3): 355–62.

Gordon, T. (1974) *T.E.T. Teacher Effectiveness Training*, New York: Wyden.

Goswami, U. (2001) Cognitive development – no stages, please – we're British, *British Journal of Psychology*, 92: 257–77.

Gray, J., Hussey, S., Schagen, I. and Charles, M. (2003) The primary side of the transfer divide: heads' perceptions and pupil progress, in Galton, M., Gray, J. and Rudduck, J. (eds) *Transfer and Transitions in the Middle Years of Schooling (7–14): Continuities and Discontinuities in Learning*, Research Report 443, Nottingham: Department for Education and Skills (DfES).

Gray, J., Hopkins, D., Reynolds, D., Farrell, S. and Jesson, D. (1999) *Improving Schools: Performance and Potential*, Buckingham: Open University Press.

Hacker, D. (1998) Definitions and empirical foundations, in Hacker, D., Dunlosky, J. and Graesser, A. (eds) *Metacognition in Educational Theory and Practice*, Hillsdale, NJ: Lawrence Erlbaum.

Hall, E. (1994) The social relational approach, in Kutnick, P. and Rogers, C. (eds) *Groups in Schools*, London: Cassell.

Halpern, D. (1998) Teaching critical thinking for transfer across domains, *American Psychologist*, 53 (4): 449–55.

Halpern, D. (2002) *Thinking Critically about Critical Thinking* 4th edn, Mahwah, NJ: Lawrence Erlbaum.

Handy, C. (1993) *Understanding Organisations* 4th edn, London: Penguin.

Hardman, F., Smith, F. and Wall, K. (2003) Interactive whole class teaching in the national literacy strategy, *Cambridge Journal of Education*, 33 (2): 197–215.

Hargreaves, A. (1992) Cultures for teaching: a focus for change, in Hargreaves, A. and Fullan, M. (eds) *Understanding Teacher Development*, London: Cassell in association with Teachers College Press, Columbia University, New York.

Hargreaves, A. (2000) Mixed emotions: teachers' perceptions of their interactions with students, *Teaching and Teacher Education*, 16: 811–26.

Hargreaves, A. (2001) Emotional geographies of teaching, *Teachers College Record*, 103 (6): 1056–80.

Hargreaves, L., Moyles, J., Merry, R., Patterson, F., Pell, A. and Esarte-Sarries, V. (2003) How do primary school teachers define and implement interactive teaching in the national literacy strategy in England?, *Research Papers in Education*, 18 (3): 217–36.

Harlen, W. and Malcolm, H. (1999) *Setting and Streaming: A Research Review*, Edinburgh: Scottish Council for Research in Education (SCRE).

Harnischfeger, A. and Wiley, D. (1978) Conceptual issues in models of school learning, *Curriculum Studies*, 10 (3): 215–31.

Harrop, A. and Swinson, J. (2000) Natural rates of approval and disapproval in British infant, junior and secondary classrooms, *British Journal of educational Psychology*, 70: 473–83.

Harter, S. (1981) A new self-report scale of intrinsic versus extrinsic orientation in the classroom: motivational and informational components, *Developmental Psychology*, 17, 300–12.

Hastings, N. and Chantry, K. (2002) *Reorganising Primary School Learning*, Buckingham: Open University Press.

Hastings, N. and Schweiso, J. (1995) Tables and tasks: the effects on seating arrangements on task engagement in primary classrooms, *Educational Researcher*, 37 (3): 279–91.

Hastings, N., Schweiso, J. and Wheldall, K. (1996) A place for learning, in Croll, P. and Hastings, N. (eds) *Effective Primary Teaching: Research Based Classroom Strategies*, London: David Fulton.

Hattie, J. (2002) *The Power of Feedback for Enhancing Learning*, Paper given to an ESRC sponsored seminar on Thinking Skills, April, University of Newcastle upon Tyne.

Hilsum, S. and Cane, B. (1971) *The Teacher's Day*, Slough: National Foundation of Educational Research (NFER).

Hirst, P. (1968) The contribution of philosophy to the study of the curriculum, in Kerr, J. (ed.) *Changing the Curriculum*, Leicester: Leicester University Press.

Holland, J. (1996) *The Psychology of Vocational Choice*, Waltham, MA: Blaisdell.

Holt, J. (1984) *How Children Fail*, London: Penguin.

Howe, C. and Tolmie, A. (2003) Group working primary school science: discussion, consensus and guidance from experts, *International Journal of Educational Research*, 39 (1) 15–17.

Hummel, J. and Holyoake, K. (1997) Distributed representations of structure: a theory of analogical access and mapping, *Psychological Review*, 104: 427–66.

Jarvis, T. and Pell, A.W. (2002) Effect of challenger experience on elementary school children's attitudes to science, *Journal of Research in Science Teaching*, 39 (10): 979–1000.

Johnson, D. and Johnson, F. (2000) *Joining Together: Group Theory and Group Skills* 7th edn, Boston, MA: Allyn and Bacon.

Johnson, D.W. and Johnson, R.T (1985) The internal dynamics of cooperative learning groups, in Slavin, R., Sharan, S., Kagan, S., Hertz-Lazarowitz, R., Webb, N. and Schmuck, R. (eds) *Learning to Cooperate, Cooperating to Learn*, New York: Plenum, pp. 103–24.

Johnson, D.W. and Johnson, R.T (1987) *Learning Together and Alone: Co-operative, Competitive and Individualistic Learning*, Englewood Cliffs, NJ: Prentice-Hall.

Johnson, D.W., Johnson, R.T. and Maruyama, G. (1983) Interdependence and interpersonal attraction among heterogeneous and homogeneous individuals: a theoretical formulation and a meta-analysis of the research, *Review of Educational Research*, 53 (1): 5–54.

Joyce, B. and Weil, M. (1972) *Models of Teaching* 2nd edn, Englewood Cliffs, NJ: Prentice-Hall.

Joyce, B., Calhoun, E. and Hopkins, D. (1997) *Models of Learning – Tools for Teaching*, Buckingham: Open University Press.

Kagan, S. (1988) *Cooperative Learning: Resources for Teachers*, Riverside, CA: University of California Press.

Kast, A. and Conner, K. (1988) Sex and age differences in response to informational and controlling feedback, *Personality and Social Psychology Bulletin*, 14: 514–23.

King, A. (1992) Facilitating elaborative learning through guided student generated questioning, *Educational Psychologist*, 27: 89–118.

Kingsley-Mills, C., McNamara, S. and Woodward, L. (1992) *Out from Behind the Desk: A Practical Guide to Groupwork Skills and Processes*, Glenfield: Leicestershire County Council.

Kulhavy, R. (1977) Feedback in written instructions, *Review of Educational Research*, 47 (1): 211–32.

Kurlick, J. and Kurlick, C. (1988) Timing of feedback and verbal learning, *Review of Educational Research*, 58 (1): 79–97.

Kutnick, P. and Kington, A. (2005) Children's friendships and learning in school: cognitive enhancement through social interaction?, *British Journal of Educational Psychology*, 75 (1): 1–19.

Kutnick, P. and Manson, I. (1998) Social life in the classroom: towards a relational concept of social skills for use in the classroom, in Campbell, A. and Muncer, S. (eds) *The Social Child*, Hove: Psychology Press.

Kutnick, P., Blatchford, P. and Baines, E. (2002) Pupil groupings in primary school classrooms: sites for learning and social pedagogy?, *British Educational Research Journal*, 28 (2): 189–208.

Kutnick. P., Hodgkinson, S., Sebba, J., Humphreys, S., Galton, M., Steward, S., Blatchford, P. and Baines, E. (2006) *Pupil Grouping Strategies and Practices at Key Stages 2 and 3: Case Studies of 24 Schools in England*, Research Report 796, Nottingham: DfES.

Kutnick, P., Sebba, J., Blatchford, P., Galton, M. and Thorp, J. with MacIntyre, H. and Berdondini, L. (2005) *The Effects of Pupil Grouping: Literature Review*, Research Report 688, Nottingham: DfES.

Kyriacou, C. and Golding, M. (2004) *A Systematic Review of the Daily Mathematics Lesson in Enhancing Pupil Confidence and Competence in Early Mathematics*, A review conducted for the Evidence for Policy and Practice Information (EPPI) and Coordination Centre, University of London Institute of Education.

Lahelma, E., and Gordon, T. (1997) First day in secondary school: learning to be a 'professional pupil', *Educational Research and Evaluation*, 3(2): 119–39.

Laslett, R. and Smith, C. (1984) *Effective Classroom Management*, London: Croom Helm.

Lave, J. and Wenger, E. (1999) Learning and pedagogy in communities of practice, in Leach, J. and Moon, B. (eds) *Learners and Pedagogy*, Buckingham: Open University Press.

Leach, J. and Moon, B. (1999) Recreating pedagogy, in Leach, J. and Moon, B. (eds) *Learners and Pedagogy*, Buckingham: Open University Press.

Leo, E. and Galloway, D. (1996) Conceptual links between cognitive acceleration through science education and motivational style: a critique of Adey and Shayer, *International Journal of Science Education*, 18 (1): 35–49.

Light, P. and Littleton, K. (1994) Cognitive approaches to group work, in Kutnick, P. and Rogers, C. (eds) *Groups in Schools*, London: Cassell.

Lightfoot, L. (1997) Help squads for 18 worst schools, *Electronic Telegraph* Issue 726, 21 May.

Lipman, M., Sharp, A. and Oscanyan, F. (1980) *Philosophy in the Classroom*, Philadelphia, PA: Temple University Press.

Locke, E. and Latham, G. (1990) *A Theory of Goal-setting and Task Performance*, Englewood Cliffs, NJ: Prentice-Hall.

Lortie, D. (1975) *Schoolteacher*, Chicago, IL: University of Chicago Press.

MacBeath, J. and Galton, M. (2004) *A Life in Secondary Teaching: Finding Time for Learning*, London, NUT.

MacBeath, J. and McGlynn, A. (2002) *Self Evaluation: What's in it for Schools?* Abingdon: RoutledgeFalmer.

MacBeath, J., Galton, M., Steward, S., MacBeath, A. and Page, C. (2006) *The Costs of Inclusion: A Study of Inclusion Policy and Practice in English Primary, Secondary and Special Schools*, University of Cambridge: Faculty of Education for the National Union of Teachers (NUT).

MacDonald, A., Meill, A. and Mitchell, L. (2002) An investigation of children's musical collaborations: the effect of friendship and age, *Psychology of Music*, 30 (2): 148–63.

Marsh, H. (1989) Age and sex effects in multiple dimensions of self-concept: pre-adolescence to early adulthood, *Journal of Educational Psychology*, 81: 417–30.

McCallum, B., Hargreaves, E. and Gipps, C. (2002) Learning: the pupil's voice, *Cambridge Journal of Education*, 30 (2): 275–89.

McGuinness, C. (1999) *From Thinking Skills to Thinking Classrooms: A Review and Evaluation of Approaches for Developing Pupils' Thinking Skills*, DfEE Research Report RR115, Nottingham: Department for Education and Employment.

McGuinness, C. (2000) ACTS: a methodology for teaching thinking skills, *Teaching Thinking*, 2 (1): 1–12.

McGuinness, C., Curry, C., Greer, B., Daly, P. and Slaters, S. (1997) Final report on the ACTS (Activating Children's Thinking Skills) project, Phase 2, Belfast: Northern Ireland Council for Curriculum Examination and Assessment.

McLellan, R. (2006) The impact of motivational 'world-view' on engagement in a cognitive acceleration programme, *International Journal of Science Education*, 28 (7): 781–819.

Meadows, S. (1993) *The Child as a Thinker: The Development and Acquisition of Cognition in Childhood*, Abingdon: Routledge.

Mercer, N. (2000) *Words and Minds: How we use Language to Think Together*, Abingdon: Routledge.

Mercer, N., Wegerif, R. and Dawes, L. (1999) Children's talk and the development of reasoning in the classroom, *British Educational Research Journal*, 25 (1): 95–111.

Mercer, N., Dawes, L., Wegerif, R. and Sams, C. (2004) Reasoning as a scientist: ways of helping children to use language to learn science, *British Educational Research Journal*, 30 (3): 359–77.

Merry, R. (1997) Cognitive development 7–11, in Kitson, N. and Merry, R. (eds) *Teaching in the Primary School: A Learning Relationship*, Abingdon: Routledge.

Midgley, C. and Urdan, T. (1992) The transition to middle level schools: making it a good experience, *Middle School Journal*, 24: 5–13.

Miliband, D. (2004) Personalised learning: building a new relationship with schools, Speech by the Minister of State for School Standards, North of England Education Conference, Belfast, 8 January.

Moore, P. and Scevak, J. (1995) The effects of strategy training on high school science students learning from science texts, *European Journal of Psychology of Education*, 10 (4): 401–9.

Moseley, D., Elliott, J., Gregson, M. and Higgins, S. (2005) Thinking skill frameworks for use in education and training, *British Educational Research Journal*, 31 (3): 367–90.

Moyles, J. (1989) *Just Playing? The Role and Status of Play in Early Childhood Education*, Buckingham: Open University Press.

Mueller, C. and Dweck, C. (1998) Praise for intelligence can undermine children's motivation and performance, *Journal of Personality and Social Psychology*, 75 (1): 33–52.

National Advisory Committee on Creative and Cultural Education (1999) *All Our Futures: Creativity, Culture and Education*, London: DfES.

Natriello, G. and Dornbusch, S. (1985) *Teachers' Evaluative Standards and Student Effort*, New York: Longman.

Neill, S. (1991) *Classroom Non-verbal Communication*, Abingdon: Routledge.

Newmann, F. (1990) Qualities of thoughtful social studies classes: an empirical profile, *Journal of Curriculum Studies*, 22: 253–75.

Newmann, F. (ed.) (1992) *Student Engagement and Achievement in American Secondary Schools*, New York: Teachers College Press.

Newton, D. (2000) *Teaching for Understanding*, Abingdon: RoutledgeFalmer.

Nicholls, S. and Berliner, D. (2005) *The Inevitable Corruption of Indicators and Educators through High Stakes Testing*, Education Policy Research Unit (EPSL–0503–101–EPRU), Tempe, AZ: Arizona State University.

Noice, T. and Noice, H. (1997) *The Nature of Expertise in Professional Acting: A Cognitive View*, Mahwah, NJ: Lawrence Erlbaum.

NUT/NCA (2002) *Creativity in Education*, A report of a jointly sponsored conference by the National Union of Teachers and the National Campaign for the Arts held at Tate Britain and the London Institute, Wednesday, 3 July.

Nuthall, G. (2000) The role of memory in the acquisition and retention of knowledge in science and social studies units, *Cognition and Instruction*, 18 (1): 83–139.

Nuthall, G. (2004) Relating classroom teaching to student learning: a critical analysis of why research has failed to bridge the theory–practice gap, *Harvard Educational Review*, 74 (3): 273–306.

Nuthall, G. and Alton-Lee, A. (1993) Predicting learning from student experience of teaching: a theory of student knowledge construction in classrooms, *American Educational Research Journal*, 30 (4): 799–840.

Nuthall, G. and Alton-Lee, A. (1995) Assessing classroom learning: how students use their knowledge and experience to answer classroom achievement test questions in science and social studies, *American Educational Research Journal*, 32 (1): 165–223.

Ofsted (2002a) *The Curriculum in Successful Primary Schools*, London: Office for Standards in Education.

Ofsted (2002b) *The National Literacy Strategy: The First Four Years, 1998–2002*, London: Office for Standards in Education.

Ofsted (2002c) *The National Numeracy Strategy: The First Three Years, 1999–2002*, London: Office for Standards in Education.

Ofsted (2004) *Annual Report of Her Majesty's Chief Inspector of Schools 2003–4*, London: The Stationery Office.

Palincsar, A. and Brown, A. (1984) Reciprocal teaching of comprehension-fostering and comprehension-monitoring activities, *Cognition and Instruction*, 1 (2): 117–75.

Palincsar, A. and Herrenkohl, L. (1999) Designing collaborative contexts: lessons from three research programs, in O'Donnell, A. and King, A. (eds) *Cognitive Perspectives on Peer Learning*, Mahwah, NJ: Lawrence Erlbaum.

Paris, G. and Winograd, P. (1990) Promoting Metacognition and Motivation of Exceptional Children, *Remedial and Special Education*, 11 (6): 7–15.

Pintrich, P. (2002) The role of metacognition knowledge in learning, teaching and assessing, *Theory into Practice*, 41 (4): 219– 25.

Pollard, A. (1985) *The Social Word of the Primary Classroom*, London: Holt, Rinehart and Winston.

Pollard, A. and Triggs, P. with Broadfoot, P., McNess, E. and Osborn, M. (2000) *What Pupils Say: Changing Policy and Practice in Primary Education*, London: Continuum.

Putnam, R. and Borko, H. (1997) Teacher learning: implications for new views on cognition, in Biddle, B., Good, T. and Goodson, I. (eds) *The International Handbook of Teachers and Teaching*, Dordrecht, Netherlands: Kluwer.

Putnam, J., Markovchick, K., Johnson, D. and Johnson, R. (1996) Cooperative Learning and peer acceptance of pupils with learning disabilities, *Journal of Social Psychology*, 136, 741–52.

Reynolds, D. (2000) Should pedagogical change be mandated at times?, *Journal of Educational Change*, 1 (2): 193–8.

Reynolds, D. and Farrell, S. (1996) *Worlds Apart? A Review of International Surveys of Achievement Involving England*, London: HMSO.

Rogers (1991) *You Know the Fair Rule: Strategies for Making the Hard Job of Discipline in School Easier*, Harlow: Longman.

Rosenshine, B. (1979) Content, time and direct instruction, in Peterson, P. and Walberg, H. (eds) *Research on Teaching Concepts, Findings and Implications*, Berkeley, CA: McCutchan.

Rosenshine, B. (1987) Direct instruction, in Dunkin, M. (ed.) *Teaching and Teacher Education*, Oxford: Pergamon.

Rosenshine, B., Meister, C. and Chapman, S. (1996) Teaching students to generate questions: a review of intervention studies, *Review of Educational Research*, 66 (2): 181–221.

Roth, K. (2002) Talking to understand science, in Brophy, J. (ed.) *Social Constructivist Teaching: Affordances and Constraints*, New York: Elsevier.

Rowe, M. (1986) Wait time: slowing down may be a way of speeding up, *Journal of Teacher Education*, 37 (1): 43–50.

Rudduck, J. (2002) The transformative potential of consulting young people about teaching, learning and schooling, *Scottish Education Review*, 34 (2): 123–37.

Rudduck, J. (2003) Consulting pupils about teaching and learning, in *Learning Texts*, Nottingham: National College for School Leadership (NCSL).

Rudduck, J. Chaplin, R. and Wallace, G. (1996) *School Improvement, What Can Pupils Tell Us?* London: David Fulton.

Rudduck, J. and Flutter, J. (2004) *How to Improve your School: Giving Pupils a Voice*, London: Continuum.

Ryan, A. and Pintrich, P. (1977) Should I ask for help? The role of motivation and attitudes in adolescents' help seeking in math class, *Journal of Educational Psychology*, 89: 329–41.

Salomon, G. and Perkins, D. (1989) Rocky roads to transfer: rethinking mechanisms of a neglected phenomenon, *Educational Psychology*, 24: 113–42.

Sammons, P. (1995) Gender, ethnic and socio-economic differences in attainment and progress: a longitu-dinal analysis of student achievement over 9 years, *British Educational Research Journal*, 21 (4): 465–86.

Sammons, P., Hillman, J. and Mortimore, P. (1994) *Key Characteristics of Effective Schools: A Review of School Effectiveness Research*, London: Office for Standards in Education (Ofsted).

Sammons, P., Nuttall, D. and Cuttance, P. (1993) Differential school effectiveness: results from a re-analysis of the Inner London Education Authority Junior School Project data, *British Educational Research Journal*, 19 (3): 381–405.

Schon, D. (1987) *Educating the Reflective Practitioner*, San Francisco, CA: Jossey-Bass.

Schunk, D. (1983) Ability versus effort attributional feedback: differential effects on self-efficacy and achievement, *Journal of Educational Psychology*, 75: 848–56.

Sharan, N.S. (1980) Cooperative learning in small groups: recent methods and effects on achieve-ment, attitudes and ethnic relations, *Review of Educational Research*, 50 (4): 241–71.

Sharan, Y. and Sharan, S. (1992) *Expanding Cooperative Learning through Group Investigation*, New York: Teachers College Press.

Shayer, M. (1997) Piaget and Vygotsky: a necessary marriage for effective educational intervention, in Smith, L., Dockrell, J. and Tomlison, P. (eds), *Piaget, Vygotsky and Beyond*, Abingdon: Routledge.

Sheppard, J. (1993) Productivity loss in performance groups: a motivational analysis, *Psychological Bulletin*, 113 (1): 67–81.

Shulman, L. (1986) Those who understand: knowledge growth in teaching, *Educational Researcher*, 15 (2): 4–14.

Shulman, L. (1987) Knowledge and teaching: foundations of the new reform, *Harvard Educational Review*, 57 (1): 1–22.

Simco, N. (1995) Using activity analysis to investigate primary classroom environments, *British Educational Research Journal*, 21 (1): 49–60.

Simon, B. (1981) Why no pedagogy in England?, in Simon, B. and Taylor, W. (eds) *Education in the Eighties: The Central Issues*, pp. 124–45. London: Batsford.

Slavin, R.E. (1983) When does cooperative learning increase student achievement?, *Psychological Bulletin*, 94 (3), 429–45.

Slavin, R. (1995) *Cooperative Learning: Theory, Research and Practice* 2nd edn, Boston, MA: Allyn and Bacon.

Smith, F., Hardman, F., Wall, K. and Mroz, M. (2004) Interactive whole class teaching in the national literacy and numeracy strategies, *British Educational Research Journal*, 30 (3): 395–412.

Smith, G. (2002) Thinking skills: the question of generality, *Journal of Curriculum Studies*, 34: 659–78.

Smith, L. (1995) Comment on Vygotsky's criticisms of language and thought of the child and judge-ment and reasoning in the child, by Jean Piaget (translated by Leslie Smith), *New Ideas in Psychology*, 13 (3): 325–40.

Smith, L. (1999) What exactly is constructivism in education?, *Studies in Science Education*, 33: 149–60.

Sternberg, R. (2003) What is an expert student?, *Educational Researcher*, 32 (8): 5–9.

Swartz, R. and Parks, S. (1994) *Infusing Critical and Creative thinking into Content Instruction: Selections from the Elementary and Secondary Lesson Design Handbooks*, Forest Grool, CA: Critical Thinking Press and Software.

Thompson, T. (1997) Do we need to train teachers to administer praise? Self-worth theory says we do, *Learning and Instruction*, 7 (1): 49–63.

TLRP (2006) *Personalised Learning: A Commentary by the Teaching and Learning Research Programme*, at www.tlrp.org/documents/personalised_learning_pdf

Tomlinson, S. (2005) *Education in a Post-welfare Society* 2nd edn, Maidenhead: Open University Press/McGraw-Hill.

Tunstall, P. and Gipps, C. (1996) Teacher feedback to young children in formative assessment: a typology, *British Educational Research Journal*, 22 (4): 389–404.

Tymms, P. (2004) Are standards rising in English primary schools?, *British Educational Research Journal*, 30(4): 477–94.

Tymms, P. and Coe, R. (2003) Celebrating of the success of distributed research with schools: the CEM Centre, Durham, *British Educational Research Journal*, 29 (5): 639–54.

Tymms, P. and Fitz-Gibbon, C. (2001) Standards, achievement and educational performance: a cause for celebration?, in Phillips, R. and Furlong, J. (eds) *Education, Reform and the State: 25 Years of Politics, Policy and Practice*, Abingdon: Routledge.

Walford, G. (2005) Introduction: education and the Labour Government, *Oxford Review of Education*, 31 (1): 3–9.

Watkins, C. (2003) *Learning: A Sense-maker's Guide*, London: Association of Teachers and Lecturers (ATL).

Watkins, C. (2005) *Classrooms as Learning Communities: What's in it for Schools?* Abingdon: Routledge.

Watkins, C. and Wagner, P. (2000) *Improving School Behaviour*, London: Paul Chapman Publishing.

Watkins, D. and Mortimore, P. (1999) Pedagogy: what do we know?, in Mortimore, P. (ed.) *Understanding Pedagogy and its Impact on Learning*, London: Paul Chapman Publishing.

Webb, L. (2001) *Communicating*, Economic and Social Research Council (ESRC) Project Network Newsletter (2): 1.

Webb, N. (1985) Student interaction and learning in small groups: a research summary, in Slavin, R., Sharan, S., Kagan, S., Hertz-Lazarowitz, R., Webb, N. and Schmuck, R. (eds) *Learning to Cooperate, Cooperating to Learn*, New York: Plenum.

Webb, N. (1989) Peer interaction and learning in small groups, *International Journal of Educational Research*, 13: 21–39.

Webb, N. and Mastergeorge, A. (2003) Promoting effective helping behaviour in peer directed groups, *International Journal of Educational Research*, 39 (1–2): 79–97.

Webb, R. and Vulliamy, G. (2006) *Coming Full Circle? The Impact of New Labour's Education Policies on Primary School Teachers' Work*, London: Association of Teachers and Lecturers (ATL).

Webster, A. Beveridge, M. and Reed, M. (1995) *Managing the Literacy Curriculum: How Schools can become Communities of Readers and Writers*, Abingdon: Routledge.

Weiner, B. (1992) *Human Motivation: Metaphors, Theory and Research*, London: Sage.

White, J. (2006) Individualised learning? Let's cut the conclusion, *Times Educational Supplement*, News & Opinion section, 7 July.

Winne, P. and Butler, D. (1994) Student cognition in learning from teaching, in Husen, T. and Postlewaite, T. (eds) *International Encyclopaedia of Education* 2nd edn, Oxford: Pergamon.

Wood, P. (1998) *How Children Think and Learn* 2nd edn, Oxford: Blackwell.

Woods, P. (1996) *Researching the Art of Teaching*, Abingdon: Routledge.

Woods, P., Jeffery, B., Thomas, G. and Boyle, M. (1997) *Restructuring Schools, Reconstructing Teachers*, Buckingham: Open University Press.

Woodward, W. (2003) Ex-head jailed for exam forgery, *Guardian*, 8 March, www.education.guardian. co.uk/schools/story/0,,90010,00.html

Zeidner, M., Boekaerts, M. and Pintrich, P. (2000) Self-regulation: directions and challenges for future research, in Boekaerts, M., Pintrich, P. and Zeidner, M. (eds) *Handbook of Self-regulation*, London: Academic Press.

Index

active listening, 101–2
Alexander, Patricia, 32, 35, 41–3, 50–1, 69, 74, 88
Alexander, Robin, 6–9, 15, 25, 27–8, 34–6, 39, 42, 62–3, 65, 74
Alton-Lee, Adrienne, 36, 53–4, 56, 59
ambiguity, 43, 79–84, 121, 108
assertive discipline, 115–16
assessment, 16, 19, 91–2
assessment
 for learning, 86, 92, 125–6
 peer, 92
 self, 86
 structured, 23
attitudes
 deterioration in, 28
 pupils' 20, 21–3
 to science, 74
 of teachers, 12

behaviour and learning, 114–17
Berliner, David, 18, 21, 35, 42–3
Blatchford, Peter, 94, 104, 108
Brophy, Jere, 49, 51, 58–9, 60, 67, 69, 78, 85–6
Brown, Anne, 15, 38, 40–1, 66, 73, 76

child-centred approaches, 3, 125
classroom organisation, 24–8
cognitive conflict, 49
communication, 8, 39
communication
 non-verbal, 109–10
 one-way, 62
 skills, 99–101, 104
 spoken and written, 32, 38
constructivism, 17, 37–8, 40, 45
constructivism
 social, 38, 97

cooperative learning 68, 94, 96
craft knowledge, 6–7, 10, 30, 44

Desforges, Charles, 6–7, 30, 34, 59
DfES (Department for Education and Skills), 15–16, 30, 124–6
direct instruction, 10, 57–8, 61–2, 67–8, 72, 77–8, 89, 91, 94, 104–5
discipline knowledge, 6, 10, 33
Doyle, Walter, 78–9, 81, 108
Dweck, Carol, 23, 86

emotional geographies in teaching, 111–14
Entwistle, Noel, 23, 40, 52, 96
Excellence and Enjoyment, 15, 30
Excellence in Cities, 14
Excellence in Schools, 14, 16, 29
expert
 group person, 105
 learners, 88
 thinkers, 3, 43
 performance, 42, 45, 52
 problem solver, 41, 4
expertise, 71, 76
expertise
 and intuition, 43–5
 developing, 40–2
explaining, 66–7

feedback, 84–9
flow, 50–1

Galton, Maurice, 7, 11, 13, 18, 19–20, 25, 27, 31, 60, 62, 66, 68, 74, 77–8, 84–5, 95–7, 106, 108, 112–13, 115,119, 124
Gardner, Howard, 42, 51–2, 68, 118–19
generic
 question stems, 66

schema, 59
skills, 120–1
Gray, John, 17–18, 117
group
    decision making, 102–3
    rules, 98
    size, 106
group work, 59, 63–4, 66–7, 94–110, 114, 120, 122, 124–5,
groupwork
    and teacher interaction, 108–10
    as a neglected art, 68
    key ideas, 96–7
    suitable tasks, 107–8
    training, 97–9

handling conflict, 103–5
Hargreaves, Andy, 8, 11, 111–12, 114
Hargreaves, Linda, 25–6
Hattie, John, 84–5, 87–9

ICT (information communications technology), 126
individualised
    approaches, 14, 125
    learning, 126
information processing, 35–6
intelligence
    artificial, 41
    emotional, 111
    tests, 57, 118

knowledge
    and understanding, 50
    application, 52
    commonplace, 55
    conceptual, 32, 47
    conditional, 32
    construction, 59
    craft, 6–7, 10, 44
    declarative, 32
    frameworks, 32–5
    metacognitive, 32, 41, 73, 84, 108, 121
    procedural, 32, 45, 47, 51, 59, 81, 95, 121
    transformative, 52
    transmission, 49, 53, 55, 58, 88, 125
    typology, 30–2, 46
    strategic, 41, 47

Kutnick, Peter, 68, 95–7, 107, 125

learning
    as developing expertise, 40–5
    as knowledge construction, 37–8
    as information processing, 35–6
    in social–cultural contexts, 38–40
    personalised, 123–7
    styles, 31, 118–20, 125
left brain-right brain, 5
literacy and numeracy hours, 2, 15, 21, 25, 46, 67, 81, 84, 126
    strategies, 4–5, 14–16, 24–5, 27–8, 57, 123
    task force, 14–15

MacBeath, John, 11, 16, 18, 20, 22, 27, 50, 93, 112, 115
McGuinness, Carol, 46, 69, 122
Mercer, Neil, 34, 61, 63–4, 95–6
metacognition, 52, 79, 81, 92
    and subject knowledge, 33
    as a deliberative process, 47
    definition of, 72
metacognitive
    awareness, 53, 68, 105, 121
    capacities, 73, 85
    knowledge, 32, 41, 59, 69, 84, 108, 121
    learning, 94
    processes, 46–7, 121
    skills, 77, 92
    strategies, 84
    thinking, 105
    understanding, 83, 108
    wisdom, 88, 114, 123
Moseley, David, 46–7, 87, 120–1
motivation, 7, 10, 21–2, 24, 28, 42–3, 46, 60, 78–9, 88, 119, 121, 126
    in groups, 95–96

National Curriculum, 67, 74, 88, 102
    and personalised learning, 124
    constraints, 28
    entitlement, 58
    levels, 88–9
    review of, 14
    testing, 16–18, 20, 64

New Labour, 4–5, 9, 11, 20, 28, 57
    reforms, 13–18
Nuthall, Graham, 36, 53–4, 56–7, 89

ORACLE (Observational Research and Classroom Learning), 11, 26, 67, 95

OFSTED (Office of Standards in Education) 22, 25–8,
  reviews, 5, 15
  inspections, 123

pedagogy
  appropriate, 35, 72
  classroom, 28, 52
  debate on, 3
  definition, 7
  effective, 94
  models, 49, 63
  organisational aspects, 25, 62
  primary school, 9
  recommended, 124
  scientific basis, 4, 6, 7, 10
  social, 96
  status, 10–12
Piaget, Jean, 3, 37–9, 118
primary strategy, 28, 30
pupil voice, 112–18

questioning, 57, 63
  challenging, 5, 92
  patterns, 25, 27
  rapid, 93
  strategies, 67
questions
  appropriate, 27, 66
  controlling, 114
  evaluative, 106
  helpful, 101
  how and what, 76
  open vs closed, 26–27, 60–2
  probing, 106
  social, 81
  teachers, 27, 66
  thinking, 66
  vs statements, 25

reciprocal teaching, 66, 76–7
risk
  and ambiguity, 79–84
  and challenge, 78, 88–9
Rosenshine, Barak, 10, 58, 76–7, 81

Sammons, Pamela, 72, 117
scaffolding, 28, 69, 73–5, 81, 84, 105, 110, 122
  different forms, 76–9
  in science, 74–5
  non-directed, 88, 92
self
  actualisation, 31
  assessment, 86
  awareness, 32
  confidence, 84
  evaluation, 81, 84, 92, 98, 105–6
  esteem, 10, 94, 96, 110
  image, 85, 88
  knowledge, 33
  regulation, 32, 47, 75, 84–9, 92, 120–1
Smith, Leslie, 39–40, 46
Standards Unit, 125
subject knowledge, 74

teachers' workloads, 18–20, 112
teaching
  dialogic, 62–4, 93, 115
  dichotomies, 3
  for transmission, 52–7
  for understanding, 59–60
  interactive, 4, 11, 24, 26–7, 91
  scientific approaches, 3–4
  subject knowledge, 9, 69, 74
  tailored, 124
  working theories of, 4, 36, 75
thinking skills, 46, 69, 121–3
  promoting, 108
  training, 125
time on task, 9, 98
TLRP (Teaching and Learning Research Programme), 94, 104, 126
Tymms, Peter, 17

Vygotsky, Lev, 38–40, 97

wait-time (thinking time), 64–5
Watkins, Chris, 36, 38, 44, 47–8, 69–70, 115–17, 127
Webb, Noreen, 63, 94, 96–7
Webb, Rosemary, 25–7